D0064811

The
Brussels
Griffon

An Owner's Guide To

A HAPPY HEALTHY PET

Howell Book House

Howell Book House
Macmillan General Reference
A Pearson Education Macmillan Company
1633 Broadway
New York, NY 10019-6785

Macmillan Publishing books may be purchased for business or sales promotional use.
For information, please write: Special Markets Department, Macmillan Publishing
USA, 1633 Broadway, New York, NY 10019-6785.

Library of Congress Cataloging-in-Publication Data
Vickers-Smith, Lorene.
The Brussels griffon / [Lorene Vickers-Smith].
p. cm. — (An Owner's guide to a happy healthy pet)
ISBN 1-58245-013-7

1. Brussels griffon. I. Title. II. Series.
SF429.B79V535   1999
636.76—dc21   99-22700
                                     CIP
Manufactured in the United States of America
10 9 8 7 6 5 4 3 2 1

Series Director: Amanda Pisani
Editor: Seymour Weiss
Book Design: Michele Laseau
Cover Design: Iris Jeromnimon
Illustration: Laura Robbins
Photography:
   Cover by Mary Bloom
   Ashbey Photography: 7
   Mary Bloom: i, 5, 8 bottom, 10, 11 top, 12, 13, 16, 18, 19, 20, 22, 23, 24, 26, 27, 28,
   *36–37, 38, 44, 45, 46, 47, 48, 49, 50, 52, 54, 55, 56, 57, 58, 60, 61, 62, 64, 65, 67, 69,
   71, 72, 74, 75, 79, 94*
   Janell Copas: 30, 41, 53
   Lorene Vickers-Smith: 1–2, 8 top, 11 bottom, 15, 17, 25, 29
   From The Dog's Medical Dictionary, *courtesy of Lorene Vickers-Smith:* 14
Production Team: Tammy Ahrens, Carrie Allen, Clint Lahnen, Oliver Jackson, Dennis
   Sheehan, Terri Sheehan

Contents

part one

Welcome to the World of the Brussels Griffon

1 What Is a Brussels Griffon? 5
2 The Brussels Griffon's Ancestry 13
3 The World According to the Brussels Griffon 19

part two

Living with a Brussels Griffon

4 Bringing Your Brussels Griffon Home 38
5 Feeding Your Brussels Griffon 54
6 Grooming Your Brussels Griffon 60
7 Keeping Your Brussels Griffon Healthy 72

part three

Enjoying Your Dog

8 Basic Training 98
by Ian Dunbar, Ph.D., MRCVS

9 Getting Active with Your Dog 128
by Bardi McLennan

10 Your Dog and Your Family 136
by Bardi McLennan

11 Your Dog and Your Community 144
by Bardi McLennan

part four

Beyond the Basics

12 Recommended Reading 151
13 Resources 155

Welcome
to the
World

of the

Brussels
Griffon

External Features of the Brussels Griffon

chapter 1

What Is a

Brussels Griffon?

The dog has got more fun out of Man than Man has got out of the dog, for the clearly demonstrable reason that Man is the more laughable of the two animals.

—JAMES THURBER

If the dog in Thurber's observation was a Brussels Griffon, however, the noted wit might have decided it was a toss-up. Griffons are spontaneous little outbursts of both surprise and joy. A Griffon can be depended upon to keep you on your toes, and will definitely keep you laughing.

In relation to a host of related breeds, the Brussels Griffon is a relative newcomer to the family of purebred dogs. As the name suggests, the Griffon was originally developed in Belgium, late in the nineteenth century from a combination of several other Toy dogs. It has been definitely established that the three primary breeds behind the Brussels Griffon (though there may have been more) were the Pug, the English Toy Spaniel and a small, rough coated, terrier-like, stable ratter, similar to the German Affenpinscher, which is a much older breed. From that varied ancestry, today's Brussels Griffon is a well-balanced, squarely-built, brachycephalic (flat-faced) Toy dog. It is vivacious, hardy, active and extremely intelligent. There are two coat varieties, rough and smooth, and four acceptable colors, solid red, solid black, black-and-tan and *belge* (a red ground color with a black or gray overlay on the body).

The term *Griffon* means thickly or roughly coated. To shorten the name, one would refer to the breed as a *Griffon* rather than a *Brussels* in the same sense that a German Shepherd Dog would be called a *Shepherd* and not a *German*.

WHAT IS A BREED STANDARD?

A breed standard—a detailed description of an individual breed—is meant to portray the *ideal* specimen of that breed. This includes ideal structure, temperament, gait, type—all aspects of the dog. Because the standard describes an ideal specimen, it isn't based on any particular dog. It is a concept against which judges compare actual dogs and breeders strive to produce dogs. At a dog show, the dog that wins is the one that comes closest, in the judge's opinion, to the standard for its breed. Breed standards are written by the breed parent clubs, the national organizations formed to oversee the well-being of the breed. They are voted on and approved by the members of the parent clubs.

The AKC Standard for the Brussels Griffon

In the following section, the actual text of the AKC Standard for the Brussels Griffon appears in italics. The author's commentary follows in roman type.

General Appearance *A toy dog, intelligent, alert, sturdy, with a thickset, short body, a smart carriage and set-up, attracting attention by an almost human expression. There are two distinct types of coat: rough or smooth. Except for coat, there is no difference between the two.*

This paragraph describes a small, alert, flat-faced dog that descended from a strong stable-ratter influence. He also can make a calm, loving lapdog. His large, very dark, "knowing" eyes and upturned pouty chin really do strike some people as being humanlike. Though his body is to be thickset, he should be small and compact.

From street urchin to show star—the author with her Westminster Best of Breed choice, Ch. Toobee's Rembrandt, owned by Dr. and Mrs. Harold Brooks.

Size, Proportion, Substance *Size—Weight usually 8–10 pounds, and should not exceed 12 pounds. Type and quality are of greater importance than weight, and a smaller dog that is sturdy and well proportioned should not be penalized. Proportion—Square, as measured from point of shoulder to rearmost projection of upper thigh and from wither to ground. Substance—Thickset, compact with good balance. Well boned.*

This body is thickset and compact, rather than slight bodied or terrier-type, set high on long legs.

Head *A very important feature. An almost human expression. Eyes set well apart, very large, black, prominent, and well open. The eyelashes long and black. Eyelids edged with black. Ears small and set rather high on the head. May be shown cropped or natural. If natural they are carried semierect. Skull large and round, with a domed forehead. The stop deep. Nose very black, extremely short, its tip being set back*

7

*deeply between the eyes so as to form a lay-back. The nostrils large. **Disqualifications**—Dudley or butterfly nose. **Lips** edged with black, not pendulous but well brought together, giving a clean finish to the mouth. **Jaws** must be undershot. The incisors of the lower jaw should protrude over the upper incisors. The lower jaw is prominent, rather broad with an upward sweep. Neither teeth nor tongue should show when the mouth is closed. A wry mouth is a serious fault.*

Disqualifications—*Bite overshot. Hanging tongue.*

A headstudy of a black smooth, showing beautiful breed type.

The Standard's description of the head is very explicit and the most important feature of the Brussels Griffon. **Breed type** is either found or lacking in the Griffon's head. The face gives the impression of great width for the dog's size. The head is not so wide or flat in topskull as an envelope, such as is highly desirable in a Pekingese head, but neither should it ever seem long and narrow. The Griffon's head type closely resembles that of his English Toy Spaniel ancestors, and the domed forehead is viewed in profile. The skull between the ears is slightly rounded, from the front.

The muzzle and chin should be wide to balance the broad skull. The nosepad is broad and set in line with the large, well-open, round, dark, expressive eyes, and the tip of the nose is tilted into the forehead. The nostrils should be large and well open.

A lovely head portrait of a black rough.

In profile, the bottom jaw will protrude beyond the nosepad and curve upward so that the bottom lip will meet the short upper lip. This gives the Brussels Griffon a really unique expression, and whether "human" or "monkey-like," it is both comical and intelligent to behold.

The ears of the smooth type, if left uncropped, are soft and velvety. The ears on the rough variety will grow long hair and tufts, which must be removed if the Griffon is to be tidied up. The correct natural (uncropped) ear, which is becoming quite popular, should be small and will be lifted off the forehead before it breaks to fall forward.

Neck, Topline, Body *Neck medium length, gracefully arched. Topline—Back level and short. Body—A thickset, short body. Brisket should be broad and deep, ribs well sprung. Short-coupled. Tail—set and held high, docked to about one-third.*

While the brisket should be broad, the Griffon's body should not fall away to a narrow rear. The hips are also broad enough to give the body a square appearance rather than a pear shape. A low set tail can be held so high that it will look high set and a high set tail can be held down so that it is hard to tell that the set-on (the position of the tail at its juncture with the rump) is correct. The set-on is structural but how a dog carries his tail reflects his attitude.

Forequarters *Forelegs medium length, straight in bone, well muscled, set moderately wide apart and straight from the point of the shoulders as viewed from the front. Pasterns short and strong. Feet round, small, and compact, turned neither in nor out. Toes well arched. Black pads and toenails preferred.*

Hindquarters *Hind legs set true, thighs strong and well muscled, stifles bent, hocks well let down, turning neither in nor out.*

Stifles bent means that the stifle joint (knee) of the rear leg should have a moderate bend which balances with

> ## THE AMERICAN KENNEL CLUB
>
> Familiarly referred to as "the AKC," the American Kennel Club is a non-profit organization devoted to the advancement of purebred dogs. The AKC maintains a registry of recognized breeds and adopts and enforces rules for dog events including shows, obedience trials, field trials, hunting tests, lure coursing, herding, earthdog trials, agility and the Canine Good Citizen program. It is a club of clubs, established in 1884 and composed, today, of over 500 autonomous dog clubs throughout the United States. Each club is represented by a delegate; the delegates make up the legislative body of the AKC, voting on rules and electing directors. The American Kennel Club maintains the Stud Book, the record of every dog ever registered with the AKC, and publishes a variety of materials on purebred dogs, including a monthly magazine, books and numerous educational pamphlets. For more information, contact the AKC at the address listed in Chapter 13, "Resources," and look for the names of their publications in Chapter 12, "Recommended Reading."

the bend in the shoulder (layback). The dog's hock corresponds with the human heel. The dewclaws or fifth digits, if present on any of the feet, are usually removed at birth. Occasionally a Griffon will have a dewclaw on a hind foot. If your Griffon has not had any of his dewclaws removed, you must keep them trimmed short so they don't catch on clothing or furniture, tear or the dewclaw nails grow around into the dog's foot from neglect. When the Brussels Griffon is facing away, either standing or moving, each of his hind legs should be in a straight line. The bones of either the front or rear legs of the Brussels Griffon should never seem spindly or give a fragile appearance.

Coat *The **rough coat** is wiry and dense, the harder and more wiry the better. On no account should the dog look or feel wooly, and there should be no silky hair anywhere. The coat should not be so long as to give a shaggy appearance, but should be distinctly different all over from the smooth coat. The head should be covered with wiry hair, slightly longer around the eyes, nose, cheeks, and chin, thus forming a fringe. The rough coat is hand-stripped and should never appear unkempt. Body coat of sufficient length to determine texture. The coat may be tidied for neatness of appearance, but coats prepared with scissors and/or clippers should be severely penalized. The **smooth coat** is straight, short, tight and glossy, with no trace of wiry hair.*

An example of the "belge" color phase in an uncropped female.

Color *Either 1) **Red**: reddish brown with a little black at the whiskers and chin allowable; 2) **Belge**: black and reddish brown mixed, usually with black mask and whiskers; 3) **Black**

and Tan: *black with uniform reddish brown markings, appearing under the chin, on the legs, above each eye, around the edges of the ears and around the vent; 4)* **Black:** *solid black.*

Both the smooth and the rough coats occur in all four colors. Belge seems to be a catch-all for anything between red and black. Each hair in the correct belge color is multicolored black and red, and the effect results in an overall smoky-colored coat. Often the belge will have a black face and some may carry tan points, as in the black-and-tan color. Adolescent rough Griffons may have some coarse white hairs in their coats that will usually disappear with the first thorough stripping. Often these puppies with a speckling of white hair will have excellent hard, wiry coats.

A handsome pair of black-and-tans—both rough-and smooth coated.

Any white hairs are a serious fault, except for "frost" on the muzzle of a mature dog, which is natural.

Disqualification *White spot or blaze anywhere on coat.*

Gait *Movement is a straightforward, purposeful trot, showing moderated reach and drive, and maintaining a steady topline.*

A well-built Brussels Griffon can cover ground effortlessly.

The moderate reach and drive reflect the moderate angles of the shoulder and stifle. The Griffon should not have the stilted movement of a straight-angulated Chow

Chow, nor should he have the extreme outstretched movement of a well-angulated working dog. The movement of a soundly built dog will not be choppy or jerky. The dog will move smoothly both from the side as well as coming and going. The legs will not wobble but will give the impression of strength.

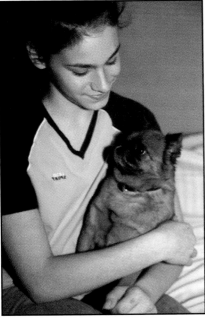

The modern Brussels Griffon is meant to be the ideal companion, and he excels at the job.

Temperament *Intelligent, alert and sensitive. Full of self-importance.*

The Brussels Griffon is one of the most highly intelligent breeds I have ever encountered. This doesn't necessarily make him easier to live with. He will think up things to do faster than you can keep up with. He is so smart that he may seem standoffish in a new situation or with new people. He hangs back and waits a minute to see what will happen next. Because of this tendency, how and where he spent his infancy is very important to his social development. The breeder should have provided scrupulously clean quarters and security to the puppy while socializing and exposing the puppy to new experiences. Griffon puppies that have only experienced a kennel life in a pen with other puppies often will have behavioral problems when moving into a home situation. A Griffon puppy that has been well socialized, might be hesitant for a few moments in a new situation, but will recover quickly and join in the fun. The Griffon is very sensitive and needs patience and very gentle handling. Griffons are devoted to their people and love praise. Praise will get results much faster than a stern correction, which may also do lasting damage.

chapter 2

The Brussels Griffon's Ancestry

The First Griffon Type Dogs

As early as the fifteenth century, small wire-coated dogs existed in many parts of Europe. These self-reliant characters were widely used as ratters in stables, outbuildings and anywhere quantities of grain were stored. We have many proofs of these dogs' antiquity in the works of art from previous centuries. A

dog that very much resembles the modern Griffon appears in the famous painting *The Marriage of Giovanni Arnolfini and Giovanna Cenami* by Jan van Eyck, dated 1434. It makes an interesting statement on human vanity, but gives us a good view of our dogs' early ancestors.

13

At that time, the forerunners of the Brussels Griffon performed an essential service by ratting. The stablemen and farmers who depended on the useful endeavors of the Griffon's forebears also found in her a sporting companion that made ratting into a competitive pastime. Those dogs may have been used for a variety of tasks by those who would not keep a dog that did not have a useful purpose.

Admirably suited to the work they did, these *Griffons D'Ecurie*, or Stable Griffons, were considerably larger than the dogs we know today. The faces of these early dogs more closely resembled the longer foreface of the Affenpinscher rather than the flat face with upturned jaw seen on the modern Griffon. This was an essential feature of working vermin dogs. By crossings to the short-faced Toy breeds to produce the Brussels Griffon, the breed lost its suitability for work, but not its gameness. The true ancestry of the Brussels Griffon is part fact/part speculation at best—as with so many other modern breeds. The Griffon was, however, known in its present form on the European continent by 1870.

An interesting group of Cope-thorne Brussels Griffons from England dating to the early twentieth century. Note that some of the dogs are cropped while others have natural ears.

Some authorities on canine genealogy have speculated on the possible variety of breeds used in the development of today's Brussels Griffon, including the Miniature Pinscher and the German Affenpinscher. The following theory appears in Henry P. Davis's *The Modern Dog Encyclopedia* (Harrisburg, Penn., Stackpole Press, 1956)

and sums up the most popular belief on the subject— "an opinion held by many early Belgian breeders was that the breed developed from crossing small terrier types with the Pug, and perhaps the Toy Spaniel. As a result of these crosses, a smooth-coated dog evolved and for a time these puppies were put down. When the Smooth coat became popular, this variety was renamed Petite Brabançon. Breed historians never question the possibility of the Pug crosses and many of these were specifically documented." Davis's theory of the wire coat and terrier influence is completely evident, and when we compare today's Brussels Griffon's head to that of the English Toy Spaniel, there is very little difference, indeed.

The breed actually became quite the rage with Belgian high society when Queen Henrietta Maria kept several. Queen Astride of the Belgians also bred many. The Belgian Royal Family possessed Griffons as far back as 1894. American-born artist Mary Cassatt also acquired a Griffon while living in Brussels in 1873 and became a great supporter of the breed.

This 1883 Mary Cassatt painting of a seated lady with Griffon shows Batty, a favorite dog of the artist.

As a result of the earliest imports to England, the Brussels Griffon made many new friends away from her native home. The British, always quick to appreciate fine dogs, took the breed to their collective heart right away. There is still a loyal core of supporters for these dogs in England.

Interestingly, the prohibition against cropping ears became the law of the land about the same time the Brussels Griffon made her initial appearance in England. As a result, British breeders have been able to perfect dogs with lovely, small, natural ears. The charm of these drop-eared *Griffons Bruxellois* (as the English call them) is infectious.

The Brussels Griffon's popularity continued until World War I when most dog fanciers in England and on the Continent turned their efforts to their own survival. Since the war, Griffons have experienced a slow, steady increase in popularity, but were seldom seen outside the world of the show ring. Until recent media exposure directed to the Griffon by its appearance in the film, *As Good As It Gets,* and the television sitcom, *Spin City,* this breed has been very jealously watched over by a relatively small, tight-knit group of enthusiasts.

With sudden attention by major media called to a breed, those who are closest to it will naturally express concern about the downside of rising popularity. In the next chapter there is a section called "A Brussels Griffon Is Not for Every Family." Please read this if you are considering a Griffon as your breed of choice. For all their charming appearance and high intelligence, these dogs have needs and demands that are normally not found among most other breeds. If after reading this book, you are more certain than ever that the Brussels Griffon is right for you, take the right steps. First, please seek out a responsible breeder, put yourself in his or her hands and when you find the right Griffon pet for you, have it spayed or neutered and enjoy your new friend for itself, not for any perceived trendiness.

This profile study clearly shows the extremely short foreface of the Brussels Griffon.

The Three Main Breeds of Origin

It is generally accepted that the three main breeds of origin for the Brussels Griffon were the Pug, the English Toy Spaniel and a rough-coated stable terrier very similar to the modern Affenpinscher. To gain the fullest appreciation for the character of the Griffon, it is very important to take note of and refer back to this chapter as you read this book. Each of these breeds brought to the present-day Brussels Griffon essential aspects of its now-established temperament and appearance. The Affenpinscher-type brought in the hard, wiry coat of the rough variety together with the characteristic black, black-and-tan, red and possibly even the "belge" (red and black grizzled) colors, high intelligence and marked terrier temperament.

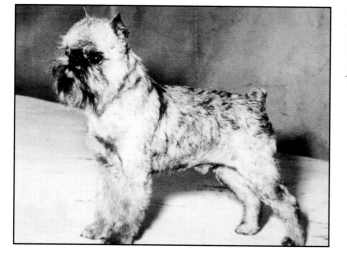

Ch. Barmere's Mighty Man, c.1959, was a top show dog and made many new friends for Brussels Griffons.

The Pug also contributed the black color, as well as its large, brachycephalic head and the short coat inherited by the Smooth variety. Both the Pug and the English Toy Spaniel contributed to the square, thickset, cobby body and sturdy bone structure, but the English Toy Spaniel set head type for the Griffon.

The ruby color phase of the English Toy Spaniel set the Griffon's deep red color; the King Charles variety was the source of the black-and-tan color.

The Griffon Becomes Established

The Belgian breeders formulated a standard by 1883 and the Griffon Bruxellois Club was formed in England in 1898. The breed was first included in the American Kennel Club (AKC) stud book in 1899. In 1908, the first Brussels Griffon champion of record was confirmed by the AKC.

Since the breed became established in the United States there has always been a moderate population, but individual quality has usually been strong. Breeders have taken pains to assure that good temperament shares the priority of good conformation. What all this means for you, the pet owner, is that the Griffon you bring into your life will look the part and act the part and be an ongoing source of joy for her entire life.

The Brussels Griffon has a long history as an ideal "people" dog.

Once the Griffon's length of foreface was bred out, the purpose of the breed shifted from vermin hunter to beloved companion and lapdog. The instinct for gameness, the will to hunt and kill rats, remains very much intact in many Griffons. Companions they are, however, and they *must* live in the middle of household activity to be truly happy.

18

chapter 3

The World
According to the
Brussels Griffon

This chapter will help you decide whether or not a Brussels Griffon is really the breed to fit into your home and life. Studying how this breed should look and act, and buying from an honest, reputable source is vitally important whether you want a house pet or a show dog. On this last point I am often asked, "Why is it important if I *only* want a house pet and am not planning to show or breed?" Actually, there is an excellent reason for studying the breed's appearance and temperament before trying to find your own Griffon.

I assume you are considering a *purebred* Brussels Griffon for your new friend and treasured family companion because specifics about this breed have caught your fancy. With a purebred dog comes the advantage of having a "blueprint" that allows you to know what to expect during the lifetime of this dog and how a certain breed *should* look and behave. How closely each individual purebred resembles this blueprint is mostly determined by the dog's breeder and his/her knowledge and ethics. The health, appearance and behavior of the Brussels Griffon that you bring home will largely depend on how well you do your homework.

Be sure the Brussels Griffon is the breed you really want before you bring a dog into your home.

For your own benefit, study the American Kennel Club (AKC) standard and interview as many breeders as it is possible for you to visit. At the same time, write the American Brussels Griffon Association (ABGA) for any information on the breed that it can send you, and a list of breeders in your area. As this book goes to press, the name and address of the current secretary appears at the end of this chapter. If there is a new ABGA secretary when you are busily engaged in seeking your ideal Griffon friend, the AKC can furnish that person's name and address upon request.

You can't be too fussy; this Griffon you will acquire will be an investment of not just your money but of the enjoyment of, hopefully, the next ten to fourteen years of your life. You won't find a perfectly healthy, letter-perfect puppy, from a perfect breeder. Perfection in every area is yet to be found in living subjects. You should be quite comfortable, however, that you have done your best to buy from a breeder whom you feel is both honest and caring. You and your veterinarian should be comfortable in the knowledge that your new puppy is happy, spunky and clean, and is starting out life with no major health problems unknown to you or the seller.

Due to the relative youth and the diverse ancestry of the Brussels Griffon, completely healthy small and large puppies can come from the same litter. However, if a puppy is quite tiny, as a precaution, have your veterinarian check him carefully for hydrocephalus and open fontanels, which is common among the tiny ones. Hydrocephalus is the technical name for water on the brain and is not uncommon among Toy breed puppies. Open fontanel is a congenital condition sometimes seen in Brussels Griffons. The fontanel is the area at the top of the skull and is normally open in newborns, fusing by about 4 weeks. The condition develops when the three bone plates of the skull fail to fuse, leaving a small hole in the skull.

Mild cases of either condition may or may not ever be a problem; however, if the breeder is not keeping the puppy until diagnosis is complete, this should definitely be reflected in the price of the dog, and the dog should only be placed in a special home with an owner who is aware that this condition may get better with age, or it may become worse, causing premature death.

A Brussels Griffon Is Not for Every Family

The Brussels Griffon has always been intended to be a companion for people. This is his sole purpose in life and he is well-suited for it. In everything he does, this bewhiskered

A DOG'S SENSES

Sight: With their eyes located farther apart than ours, dogs can detect movement at a greater distance than we can, but they can't see as well up close. They can also see better in less light, but can't distinguish many colors.

Sound: Dogs can hear about four times better than we can, *and* they can hear high-pitched sounds especially well. Their ancestors, the wolves, howled to let other wolves know where they were; our dogs do the same, but they have a wider range of vocalizations, including barks, whimpers, moans and whines.

Smell: A dog's nose is his greatest sensory organ. His sense of smell is so great he can follow a trail that's weeks old, detect odors diluted to one-millionth the concentration we'd need to notice them, even sniff out a person under water!

Taste: Dogs have fewer taste buds than we do, so they're likelier to try anything—and usually do, which is why it's especially important for their owners to monitor their food intake. Dogs are omnivores, which means they eat meat as well as vegetable matter like grasses and weeds.

Touch: Dogs are social animals and love to be petted, groomed and played with.

fellow is keenly intelligent and misses nothing. Because of this, the Griffon is not a breed for every family or every dog owner. In my opinion, the smarter a dog is, the more he gets into and the harder it is to keep ahead of him. With a Griffon, it often becomes necessary to match wits to maintain a healthy dog/owner relationship. So if you think you'd like a Griffon because he looks different or would be a novel, living ornament in your home, you would probably be better to consider some other breed.

The Brussels Griffon puppy that you add to your home will be like a perpetual 2-year-old child. Will you be able to keep up with this canine "whiz kid"?

Caring for a Brussels Griffon will be similar to caring for and protecting a 2-year-old child—a 2-year-old child that *never* grows up. He will need a great deal of positive reinforcement when he pleases you. Griffons are extremely sensitive with a definite stubborn streak. They can also *never* be "reliably" boundary trained, love to dig holes and "garden" and will leap from virtually any height (or laps and sofas) for the fun of it. They can climb over tall chain-link fences in a flash, like a monkey. They will dig tunnels under fences or squeeze through open doors between your feet, without you knowing it. Totally fearless, they have been known to clear Dutch doors with little effort. They are obedient—*most of the time*—so you may develop a false sense of security that *your* Griffon wouldn't do that, and that, of course, *your* Griffon will come *every* time you call. After all, he does have an Obedience degree! If you love your dog, save that kind of trust for something that doesn't matter as much! Griffons *need constant protection—once hurt or wronged, they will never forget it.*

Please reread the preceding paragraph and think of a 2-year-old child. Do you have the kind of energy to willingly and happily expend on this delightful little creature? If you have enough of a sense of humor to laugh rather than scream at him when he does a "catch-me-if-you-can" dance just out of your reach, if you are ready to think of his safety before anything else, at all times, then this breed could just be for you.

Sofas and Griffons go together.

The Brussels Griffon and Children

I am very careful when I let a young puppy go to a family with small children. I insist on meeting the entire family and, if possible, spending an evening with them. If the children, or adults, do not behave properly to my dogs, or if the parents do not relate properly toward their children, a puppy is a mistake for the family.

Parents must protect the puppy and gently teach the children to be considerate at the same time. Both the young puppy and small child are too immature to restrain their natural urges and also to understand the motives of the other. The Griffon does carry a terrier influence and might snap at a child who is restraining or hurting him. Only children who are old enough to understand a Griffon puppy's fragile nature must be taught the correct way to pick up or carry a puppy. (As should some adults.) Griffons can struggle to be free when one least expects it. A child might either squeeze too tightly or drop the puppy by mistake.

"Cat people" who acquire a Griffon are a special concern. A Griffon will climb up and lay on a favorite person's shoulder, very much like a cat. It is hard to get a cat person to urgently understand that she *must* keep a hand on the sleeping puppy because when he opens his eyes, he may jump, and unlike a cat, the Griffon will hurt himself. A puppy should never be put on furniture until he can climb up himself and is big enough to jump down without the possibility of injury.

When children have supervised playtime with the puppy, they should be made to sit on the floor and let the puppy crawl about on their lap. There was a time in my career as a breeder when a family with small children would never get a dog from me, period.

I was a bit overreactive to rule out all families with children from becoming candidates for owning my dogs. If a child is so inclined, pets bring out the very best sensitive feelings, *but they must be watched!* I have received rescue dogs with rubber bands grown into their necks. Eyes have been damaged, and dogs can be generally restrained, intimidated and made miserable by children. Please do not get a Griffon *for your child only.* Children are not little adults. If children were wise and responsible, they wouldn't need adult supervision.

There is much that is "cat-like" about the Brussels Griffon.

I have heard parents nag at a child to feed, walk, brush and otherwise care for *their* dog. That approach will only cause the child to resent the dog. Children can learn responsibility for a pet, but the adults in the family will always need to oversee. Get the dog *for the family,* care for him when the child is not in the mood and enjoy the loving nature that he will bring out in your child, if your child genuinely likes animals.

The Griffon's terrier ancestry gives him a sense of adventure. A snowdrift can be a special pleasure.

Brussels Griffons Need Special Attention

Are *you* ready for a dog? Are you settled in your life to the point that you spend most of your evenings at home, or go places where your Brussels Griffon would also be safe and welcome? When you are at work, or otherwise away from home, are other members of your household responsible enough to watch all of the doors and consider your Griffon's safety above everything else? Are your children small, or difficult to control, so that they will insist on carrying the puppy around, or squeezing him too tightly? Can you willingly spend the time for daily and weekly grooming and training, along with quality time to provide him with love, companionship and exercise? Are you ready for the expense and time it takes to hire a groomer for the rough coat? Will the expense of his health and dental care, or an emergency such as an eye injury, cause a squeeze in the family budget? Are you able to care for him, or hire someone to care for him, if he would get sick? Is giving him the attention he needs going to cause jealousy problems for your "significant other"? Is your *whole*

*Before adding a
Brussels Griffon
to your life, be
sure you can pro-
vide him with all
the creature com-
forts your new
dog will need.*

family ready and eager to participate, *protect* and love this new furry little family member?

The very worst thing you could do to a Brussels Griffon is to bring one into your family, decide he is too much for you to deal with most of the time and relegate him to the laundry room, basement, garage or shut him away in a crate. Once again, the only purpose of the Brussels Griffon is companionship. If a Griffon is not doing what he was bred to do, he will be unhappy. Unhappy dogs often become ill, either emotionally or physically. Please do not bring a dog home unless you are sure your entire family wants him. While every reputable seller will gladly take a dog back if there is a problem, it is unfair both to the dog and to the seller to begin this venture with the idea that it is probably temporary.

I find the most realistic "families" seeking the right house dog are those whose members grew up with dogs in their homes and perhaps their beds. They have no illusions of perfect, stuffed animal toys. They had their own toys stolen and chewed up, their dirty laundry wet on. (House dogs *will* help teach your children to keep the floor picked up. That is, if the child values his clothing and toys.)

Seasoned house dog owners have had to laugh when they find that a long, slimy rawhide chew has somehow gotten into their beds, or they tramp on a hard bone with bare feet in the middle of the night. They know that even the best trained Griffon may throw up on the new sofa or the oriental rug. Often, if one of the adults grew up with only outside dogs, farm dogs or no dogs, there is a somewhat exaggerated view of what life with a house dog is really like. This doesn't mean that if you are a "novice house dog owner" that you won't do a good job. Some of the very best homes that I have seen are with first-time house dog owners, or cat people who have had to switch due to cat allergies. I think the successful ones try harder. They read everything they can get their hands on and combine the right attitude with a great approach.

If your heart is set on a young puppy, you must prepare to be patient and put yourself into the breeder's hands.

A Puppy, an Older Griffon, Perhaps a Rescue?

Now that you have decided that, Yes! you DO have what it takes to be owned by a Brussels Griffon, you should give some serious thought to the age, sex, coat type and other factors about your dog that will best fit into your family.

PUPPIES

Puppies are delightful and brand-new. They are small and delicate and must be cared for as much as any infant. Most breeders will not let a Griffon go to a new home earlier than 12 weeks, so a Griffon of this age is still considered a very young baby.

They cannot control their bowels and bladder for extended periods of time. They must eat often and relieve themselves often. They might chew everything within their reach. They are learning at an extremely rapid rate and should not go to a home where they will be left alone most of the time. A Brussels Griffon left alone for much of this formative stage can become bored and destructive, introverted or shy. The dog can develop into a neurotic barker just to attract the attention of people in the home. He may decide to soil in

An older puppy offers many advantages to the would-be pet owner.

unacceptable places when you do come home. If you feel you must have a *baby* Griffon, and all of the adults in the home are out of the house during the same hours, please look into hiring a retired pet sitter that you would trust to enjoy, teach and stimulate the young puppy's senses during your absences.

OLDER PUPPIES AND TEENAGE GRIFFONS (8 MONTHS TO 18 MONTHS)

If the Griffon you are about to acquire is an adolescent, find out everything you can about his habits and routine, the words that he knows and how he relates to people. Older puppies are the best choice for supervised young children or responsible children of any age. They are still puppies, but they have larger bladder and bowel capacity as well as greater control.

Therefore, they can begin on the road to an adult feeding and housetraining routine. Griffons should be spayed or neutered (see Chapter 7, "Keeping Your Brussels Griffon Healthy") before reaching their "teens." Speak to your veterinarian and the breeder about the right age to have the surgery performed. These older puppies still act very puppyish, they still may steal and chew. They love to go places with their favorite people. They like to spend much of their time playing fetch and learning everything their owners can teach them. They are exuberant but thoughtful. They are very much like a human teen; sometimes awkward and unsure of themselves, sometimes cocky and independent. They still manage to be always wonderful!

ADULTS

Adult Griffons sometimes become available for a number of good reasons from reputable breeders. Such a person may have bred a litter from a female and then spayed her. Often, retired show dogs are available and occasionally someone will need to place an adult due to a divorce or other changes in personal circumstances. Sometimes in a multidog home, the pecking order serves to make one of the dogs miserable. Once relocated, these dogs usually make excellent pets, and within a few weeks or months you would never know the dog hadn't started out life in that home.

Adults have many advantages over puppies. They don't require a series of puppy shots. They can be left alone for longer periods of time, often with another dog or a cat for company while you work. Perhaps you want a more settled dog to enter your home, or perhaps you are not fast enough to follow a rambunctious youngster.

For a Brussels Griffon, every day brings a new adventure.

Griffons live long, so even if you are acquiring, for instance, an 8-year-old, you can expect to share many, many fun and healthy years with him, while offering him perhaps a better home than he had in the earlier part of his life. Ask any Griffon. They *deserve* to upgrade to a softer cushion and more quality time with their people, whenever possible.

RESCUE GRIFFONS

People interested in rescues need to be sensitive to the fact that these dogs are so named for a reason. Often the lower initial cost for a rescue dog soon equals or surpasses the normal cost of a dog because of the increased veterinary requirements of these animals. It is not uncommon for rescue dogs to have both physical and emotional health problems. Many have been mishandled or ostracized from family life and need special care to socialize and housetrain them. If you want a rescue Griffon, this is not meant to discourage you from your interest, but you must approach it with your eyes open.

OTCH, U-CDX Dixie D. Copas UDX, CGC, was acquired by Janell Copas as a rescue, and went on to become the breed's first Obedience Trial Champion.

Most AKC breeds are offered in rescue programs through their parent or chapter clubs. And when rescue is done properly by knowledgeable people, it is almost always a success.

Rescue dogs are usually placed in approved "foster homes" for a time to determine the problems and attributes of the individual. They can then be matched more successfully to a new home that will be a permanent one. The dogs that will not adjust to a family life and are "unadoptable" are not offered for adoption except to special people that are ready to take on the specific challenge. If your heart is generous and your arms are open to a rescue Griffon, your reward will soon become obvious in your rescue's grateful eyes.

Sex and Coat Type

As long as a male is neutered and a female is spayed, both sexes make marvelous pets. I've often felt that the girls had "more on their agenda" and that the boys are a bit better at cuddling. Then along comes a ragdoll of a little girl or an independent little guy to prove me wrong. Teen boys (and some teen girls), if they are spayed or neutered before puberty, might display some sexual tendencies for a few months. After the surgery this behavior should wane over the next several months as the puppy's hormone level decreases.

The SMOOTH coat will be similar to that of a Boston Terrier. A smooth will shed a little and will love to be brushed and fussed over. These dogs are basically quite clean. The ROUGH coat will need daily care and regular trips to a groomer (see Chapter 6, "Grooming Your Brussels Griffon"), but it is quite nonallergenic when it is cared for properly.

Extremes of the Weather

Any brachycephalic breed, without the length of nose to cool or heat the air before it hits the lungs and bronchi, will need protection from lengthy stays in extreme heat or cold. Griffons seem to withstand very warm or very cold weather better than Pugs, Bulldogs and many other flat-faced breeds. However, no dog should ever be left in a car when the warm weather is at all questionable or put in the yard in the winter on very cold days.

In the winter, the smooths will enjoy a jacket or sweater as will the roughs after being clipped. Never expose your Griffon to cold weather for several hours after a bath and then be sure that he feels completely dry around the neck. If you think he sounds stuffy or that he has a cold, take him right to your vet. As with most brachycephalic dogs, Griffons will get pneumonia easily if they should suffer a prolonged chill.

Socialization

As long as I am present, I find my Griffons ready to go anywhere and do anything. However, I haven't found the breed to be naturally social. Puppies tend to withdraw if they are not socialized as part of their early upbringing. Gentle handling and love from humans must begin in the nest, so it is important to get your puppy from a source that has socialized him properly. Griffons also can become quite fixated on one person if they are not around other people and handled by them regularly.

Once they are comfortable in their surroundings, Brussels Griffons can be quite charming to every member of the family. However, don't be surprised if your dog does pick a favorite person (often the person who feeds him or with whom he sleeps). He should be encouraged to have activities on an individual basis with all of his people to keep him from becoming obsessed with one person (and totally ignoring everyone else in the home).

Broad range socialization with other dogs is also a good idea. This breed is naturally quite protective of his people and turf. Puppy kindergarten classes run by obedience training groups and local dog clubs can be found in most cities. If you can't locate such a class, play dates with nonaggressive dog friends will help keep your Griffon on an even keel when encountering other animals during a walk with you or in any other social situation. When making selections for the "party," be sure to invite canines that are parasite-free, and have responsible owners. Introduce them one at a time per session, under strict supervision. I would suggest buying a copy of the video, *Sirius Puppy Training* by Dr. Ian Dunbar, and studying it carefully (see "More Information About Brussels Griffons" at the end of this chapter for ordering information).

Griffons have no concept about their own size and will routinely challenge much larger dogs. However, when the big guy turns and looks at them, chances are they will head for you and run right up your body for safety. Once "safe," they will resume the tongue-lashing they were giving the big guy! Do be careful if your Griffon likes to give other dogs "what for"; some Griffons proudly return to the owner with a mouthful of the big dog's hair. Many large breeds, sight hounds, Airedales and many of the smaller terrier breeds have natural prey drive—the instinct to catch and kill small animals. Your Griffon may charge any breed, even while he is on leash. It could be too late to avert a tragedy even before you realize what is happening.

Barking

A happy, well-socialized Griffon that spends ample time with his people will not usually be annoyingly noisy. If you don't want him to bark, a soft, "Shhhh, Quiet," when he does will usually stop him as long as you have been consistent with this form of control throughout his life. If you leave him home alone for longer than is kind for his age, he may bark for attention. If you shut your Griffon in his yard for extended periods and he gets bored or would rather be inside with you, he probably will bark in protest.

Problem barkers usually do so because they have been allowed to become bored. However, the terrier influence in the Griffon is stronger in some bloodlines than in others, and these usually do have more to say, seeming to use their voices just for the love of it. You will want to ask the breeder if your dog's parents are "barkers." Some Griffons, especially if there are two in the home, will get into a game of barking while running in the yard or chasing squirrels that taunt the dogs from the top of the fence. This shouldn't be a problem unless you have close neighbors who object. It is a great source of exercise and these sessions are usually brief.

If you have a problem with barking, first examine the situation and see if you yourself have created it. As a last resort (always after the "Quiet" command has been disregarded by your dog), you may wish to keep a squirt bottle filled with water handy, and while repeating the "Quiet" command in a calm voice, squirt the dog in the face. (This should *never* be used on a puppy.) This method will work, but as with any training method, you *must* be consistent with the squirt when you tell him to be quiet, or you may as well not even bother; he will have your number as quickly as a clever child! Again, you will be setting him up for you to be angry with him when the establishment of the undesirable habit is really your own fault.

Rough-and-Tumble, Ready to Go, or Shall We Nap Instead?

The Affenpinscher-type ancestor was a ratter and a wily stable dog with a rough coat. This influence in the breed brings the rough-and-tumble, ready to go, incredibly intelligent, alert, flower-digging little varmint forth in the Brussels Griffon. The Pug is a very sweet, stubborn and rather pushy, food-driven darling. The English Toy Spaniel is also very sweet, can be docile, stubborn, sensitive and is extremely devoted. All these breeds are affectionate *and highly self-important!* A proper Griffon's personality can be a blend of any or all of the typical temperaments from the breeds behind him—*but he will always be relentlessly self-important!* As long as you hold him in awe and serve his every whim, he will be pleased to spend his time doing whatever it is that you do.

You must see that he has a fenced yard to romp in, or you should take him on several good walks every day (see Chapter 4, "Bringing Your Brussels Griffon Home"). A healthy adult Griffon should have three or four daily walks on leash, and one of these should be fairly long. If you walk your Griffon in the city, be sure to wash the salt from his feet during the winter (see Chapter 6, "Grooming Your Brussels Griffon").

If the weather is chilly, the smooth and the softer-coated rough may need a sweater. On occasional frigid winter days in northern climates, you might test out a short walk and then give him the majority of his exercise by playing fetch in the house. Unfortunately, your exercise program won't benefit him as much on those "fetch days." You will need to supervise or check in on your Griffon even when you feel he is safe on the couch chewing a toy or sleeping in the grass in his escape-proof yard. (Remember, the intelligence comparison to that 2-year-old child.)

Brussels Griffons are ready for anything, as long as you are doing it with them. When they are especially tickled with themselves, they get a case of what I call the "puppy zooms"! They tuck their bottoms under and run as fast as they can all through the house or yard for no other reason than that they love life and those they share it with. Just about everyone has their own name for this delightful behavior, but whatever it is called, you will have almost as much pleasure watching as your Griffon will have zooming.

If your dog sleeps in bed with you, you will not find a better bedmate than the Griffon. Only the rare one will do much snoring; most will curl up like a cat and be out for the night, thrilled to be next to you! They are great with seniors and will quietly help with knitting or television watching. This makes them wonderful, sympathetic Therapy Dogs on visits to nursing homes. The fun-loving Griffon is equally happy romping, sleeping or sharing quiet moments on your lap. Brussels Griffons love to travel in cars and are small enough to easily fit in a carrier that stows under the seat in a plane. They are basically tidy in their habits and will be happy doing most anything at all, as long as you are with them. Always remember, Brussels Griffons were bred solely as *companions!*

More Information About Brussels Griffons

NATIONAL BREED CLUBS

AKC National Breed Club
The American Brussels Griffon Association
Denise Brusseau, Secretary
5921 159th Lane NW
Anoka, MN 55303

The National Brussels Griffon Club and The American Brussels Griffon Association
Breed Rescue
Mrs. Marjorie Simon, Chairman
25 Windermere
Houston, TX 77063-1409

BOOKS

Ball, Richard A. *The Brussels Griffon Primer.* Second printing edited by and available from Marjorie Simon, The National Brussels Griffon Club, 25 Windermere, Houston, TX 77063-1409, 1998.

Raynham, L. G. *The History and Management of the Griffon Bruxellois.* London: Scan House, 1985.

VIDEOS

American Kennel Club. *The Brussels Griffon.*

Dunbar, Ian, DVM, MRCVS. *Sirius Puppy Training,* Oakland, Calif.: James & Kenneth Publishers, 1987.

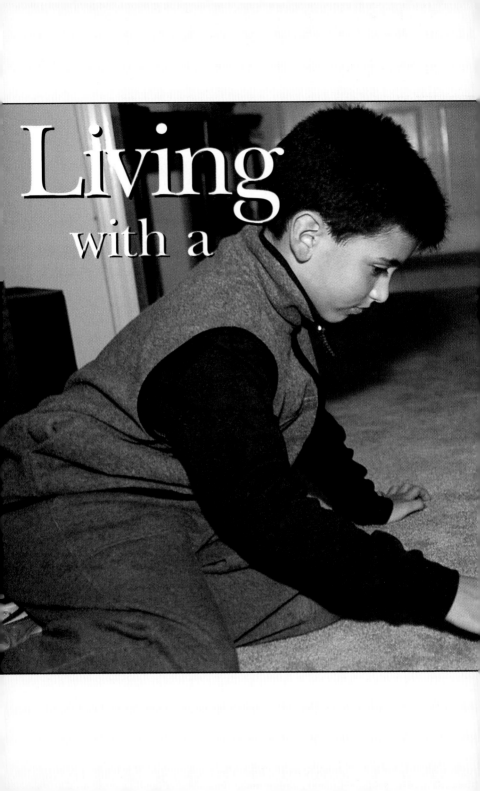

Living
with a

part two

Brussels Griffon

4

Bringing Your
Brussels Griffon
Home

When you acquire a puppy, you are making a long-term commitment that will link you, your veterinarian and the dog, from puppyhood to old age. Find yourself a veterinarian that is thoroughly familiar with flat-faced breeds (see Chapter 7, "Keeping Your Brussels Griffon Healthy"), and arrange a visit for your new Brussels Griffon, approximately a day or two after bringing her home (sooner, if you have only a twenty-four-hour health guarantee). The puppy's next shot should not be due immediately when you get her, so wait until she is comfortable and secure enough with you to visit the doctor. When you visit, take your own towel to put on the table during the examination and, if you are able to do so, hold the puppy in your arms when shots are administered.

Never bring a puppy whose next shot is past due or has had *no shots at all* into the vet's office and allow her on the floor or anywhere else that has been exposed to other animals. Be sure to ask the breeder to give you her shot and worming record, which will include the dates given, types and manufacturer of all shots. This should also include a schedule of what is yet to be given and the dates due. Show your vet the health record you were given by the breeder, and then follow your vet's advice and schedule. Do not be late for shots and chance leaving your new treasure unprotected against a possibly fatal disease. When you take your new puppy to the vet for her first examination, be sure to take a fresh stool sample to be tested for worms.

Be aware of the health guarantee that came with your Griffon, and what it provides. Generally all of your money is refunded if your vet finds major health problems and you return the dog within a short time after purchasing her. A breeder who cares about her dogs will definitely want her dogs back regardless of the problem or reason. The breeder should be available to answer your questions and help with problems for the life of your dog. Don't hesitate to call for help because the breeder may have had a similar problem and will probably know the answers.

This is also the time to think about who will care for your Griffon when you leave home for any extended period and cannot take her along. The least stressful for her would be for you to find a reliable house sitter or friend that she already knows. If this isn't possible, start interviewing and visiting boarding kennels. It will give you comfort to have the legwork already done in case you are called away unexpectedly.

What an exciting time! Your new Brussels Griffon puppy is coming home, and you will want to have your house ready for her. Call the breeder ahead of time so that you can purchase an adequate supply of the same food the puppy has been eating. You won't want to make any abrupt changes in her diet at this point. When you bring her into her new home, you will want to do so quietly, without any unnecessary fanfare, to make the transition as stress-free as possible. If she looks bewildered, you can hold her rather snugly to your body and talk gently to reassure her.

If you know how she has been living, it will go a long way to help you understand why she does what she does in her new home. Her age is very important in determining her attention span, what she is capable of learning, doing and the extent of her bladder and bowel control. Puppies that are very young (especially the smooths) should be kept above any floor drafts in a playpen.

The breeder shouldn't really permit you to take your puppy to her new home until she is around 12 weeks old, but even at that age a Griffon can be very tiny. It is not uncommon for a Griffon baby to climb right up the sides of a mesh playpen and jump out (often break-ing her front legs or hitting her head), so if you find you have a climber, you will need to make other accom-modations. You can purchase a "puppy playpen" with a lid and moveable floor, but these can be expensive for this temporary use, and you cannot reach in to pet her or tidy the pen every time you walk by. Also, square pens offer no way to set up the bed and eating area very far away from the potty area.

The floor of a small warm room in a central part of the house, near activity, or your kitchen, where she can be with you often, (NOT the basement or garage) will make a fine spot. You can buy a pressure-sensitive baby gate for the doorway so that she can still see and hear you when you are out of the room and she still won't be able to follow you. If your new Griffon puppy likes to play "monkey," you can get an extra-tall gate to dis-courage climbing. This room should be *puppy-proofed* before she arrives, and will be "home" for a while to a *young* puppy, except when she has your undivided attention during playtime in the "big house." I suggest this arrangement instead of a crate because she will need space to run around and play. She will also need to relieve herself, so in this way there will be a papered area away from her bed. Have a box of tissues and some plastic sandwich bags handy so that every time you see a stool it will be no trick to pick it right up before the puppy tramps in it.

Her bed might be a warm, soft, fluffy, polar fleece dough-nut style. Some are made with a cover over half the bed, and Griffons especially like to burrow in this type.

A young puppy should be provided with her own safe, draft-free area close to the center of household activity.

Provide *acceptable* ways to keep her occupied. For instance, she could have several puppy-proof stuffed animals for her to kill! If you visit the breeder before time to bring her home, leave a stuffed toy or small blanket so that when you bring the puppy home you also bring the toy. At this point the item will be famil-iar to the puppy and for the first few nights the new puppy will have an item to sleep with that carries the scent she is used to. Some breeders will furnish such an article from their own home for the same purpose. She can have a long work sock tied to a stationary object for her own games of tug-of-war. Remember, also, to ask for a list of words that she knows to ease the transition and reduce the puppy's stress.

She should have a bowl of clean water at all times closer to her sleeping area than her potty area. I free-feed puppies, meaning that I always have a dish of dry kibble available for puppies (see Chapter 5, "Feeding Your Brussels Griffon"). The dishes I like best for

Griffons are steep-sided heavy crocks for water. These are made in various sizes, so she can graduate to a larger crock as she grows.

Make sure any pottery or crocks you buy are made either in the U.S. or England. Glaze used on pet items from some other countries may not be as safe. These heavy water crocks work well because they do not tip over easily and it is harder for the puppy to get her feet in the bowl if she decides to take a "swim." For the dry kibble, I use the same type of crock because puppies always seem to spill their food.

Wet or moist foods are a different story. These must be fed on a flat plate with a lip so the puppy can push it against the edge and then get it in her mouth. Brachycephalic breeds have a hard time eating moist food from a bowl and they must stick their whole head down into the bowl to feed. The roughs especially do not like to have food smeared from their beard to their eyebrows (though they don't mind rolling on a dead seagull at the beach).

Time for a Walk?

Your new Brussels Griffon puppy must have a collar and leash. A young puppy will not be leash-trained and must become accustomed to something around her neck. You can use a lightweight cat collar when you are present, but you must take it off when she must be left alone, unless you can find the kind of small dog collar that has a hard rubber catch that snaps together. This type cannot tighten up if it gets caught on something.

Never use a choke chain type collar. The collar should be snug enough for you to get a couple of fingers under it for an adult, or one finger for a tiny puppy. If it is too loose, it can get caught on any projecting object, or she can slip out of it. Make a habit of sticking a finger under her collar every day when you groom or play with her to be sure it hasn't tightened up or she has not yet outgrown it.

After she is used to her collar, attach a lightweight leash to it and follow her around, coaxing her occasionally with a tidbit of food. Never pull or drag a stubborn

Griffon puppy (this is not a job for children). Keep sessions very short each day. When she is bigger and you are walking her on the beach or at a rest area, for instance, you can use a retractable lead, to give her a larger area in which to run and exercise. I would not advise this for her everyday city walks because the more distance between you and the dog, the less control you have. Your dog's collar should have both her rabies tag and an identification tag on it. You may also wish to have your Griffon microchipped (ask your veterinarian or breeder about this high-tech means of positive identification).

Always carry a few plastic sandwich bags in your pocket when you walk your dog, to pick up after her. Pull the bag over your hand, pick up the stool and turn the bag inside out, close it and drop it in the next trash receptacle.

Puppy-Proofing

Before she comes home, look at your puppy's new room from her eye level. The room should be warm and free of floor drafts. If your kitchen is to be the puppy's room, you will want to get a bottle of Grannick's® Bitter Apple and paint it on all chewable surfaces and chair rungs. Griffons are not neurotic chewers if they have other things to do and are not left alone for extended periods. Be sure all household cleaners and dangerous substances (for instance, antifreeze even in *tiny* amounts is fatal) are not available to the puppy. You need to unplug and remove all electrical cords within her reach. If a tool or appliance must be plugged in, you can attach the cord to the wall with duct tape, apply Bitter Apple and then put something heavy in front of it to assure that it is out of the puppy's reach. Be sure that anyone walking through this room will not do so in a hurry, or carelessly tramp on or accidentally kick the puppy.

Toys

Brussels Griffons of any age appreciate a wide variety of toys. Large, fluffy work socks tied in a knot are special favorites. Rubber squeak toys that the squeak cannot be chewed out of are also greatly appreciated. Stuffed animals with no eyes or parts that can be chewed off and that are finely stitched so the stuffings cannot be chewed out and choked on make safe toys that provide hours of fun.

Have a supply of toys ready before you bring your new Brussels Griffon puppy home.

Teething

One of the safest items puppies can cut their teeth on are large, *raw,* round bones. Cooked bones must be avoided as they can splinter. Remove most of the marrow because that much grease can cause diarrhea. Thin bones may chip or crack, and small bones can cause choking if the puppy would try to swallow them. A steady, lifetime habit of chewing bones, however, will wear the enamel from the teeth in adults.

In my lifetime experience with dogs, I can tell you there are no safe pieces of rawhide, ears, snouts, tails, tendons or any other animal part! My dogs, like most others, simply love them and get them as special treats, *when I am present.* If I leave the room, I pick them up! Large, solid pieces of rawhide are excellent for teething, so if you are holding your puppy and she decides to chew on your fingers, offer her a piece of rawhide and hold it for her to chew. I *am* rather fond of the clear hard rubber bones, but I have yet to interest a Griffon in one.

Training

An excellent program of dog training for all dogs appears in Chapter 8 of this book. Toy breeds, however, are very different from larger breeds, including the approach to their training. Many of the methods that would be used to train large dogs must be modified for the smaller breeds. The key to successful training is the use of common sense with each individual dog and every different breed.

Dogs are pack animals and must have a leader. Often in a Griffon household, the Griffon becomes the leader and the people become her human slaves. The Griffon is very smart and cunning, and you must keep a step ahead of her to maintain pack leadership yourself. If she gets the upper hand, she can be very demanding and it won't *always* be convenient or cute. You will find yourself mad at her, rather than at yourself for not training her properly. You must teach her from the start not to be anxious when you leave her alone for short periods, and develop all the good habits your dog should follow.

In training a Brussels Griffon, remember that the breed is very bright and that good training approaches for a large dog will not necessarily work for a Toy.

Housetraining

My attitude on housetraining is that if the puppy makes a mistake in your house, it is always your fault! The exceptions would be a rescue or a rehomed adult confused by previous poor training or lack of neutering (see Chapter 7, "Keeping Your Brussels Griffon Healthy") or a puppy raised in an unclean environment. When puppies are accustomed to living in filth, it is often extremely difficult to teach them not to soil their own bed and, later, your house.

You must be calm, clear, consistent and concise in what you expect from your new dog, if you wish to have success. It is your job to keep a constant, loving watch on your puppy every second that she is out of her own area and you put her into yours. Success depends on how clear you are in your directions and praise, and how consistent and quick you are. Puppies have very short attention spans. Her papers or the door to the outside should never be too far from where you play with her.

Do not expect a tiny Griffon puppy to go outside in the dead of winter and potty in a snowdrift. You may find one that will do it, but don't expect it. If you notice her starting to hunt a spot or circle in your house, pick her up gently and quickly and take her where you want her to go. Stand silently and patiently by, pretending to look somewhere else. She may forget what she is there for and want to play. Ignore her patiently until she remembers again and starts to use the right place. As she finishes, praise her lavishly! Take the puppy to her potty spot as often as you can. Dr. Ian Dunbar suggests once a hour, and I don't think that is too often. You must take her every time she wakes from a nap or finishes a period of strenuous exercise. You must patiently wait until she gets down to business and then she is free to play with you awhile again in "your part of the house."

When you take your puppy outside for a potty stop, be sure she is not distracted by toys or anything that would take her mind away from the real reason she is outside with you.

Transplanted adults and rescue dogs need similar training, except that they have a naturally larger holding capacity. Their attention spans, however, are still very short. Even the reputed perfectly housetrained adult, when moving to a new home, will need a variation of this training.

Crate-Training

If you purchase a crate for housetraining, it should be just large enough for the dog to stand and turn around in. This will encourage her to control her bowel and bladder longer, since natural instincts won't permit her to soil her sleeping quarters, if her cratetime is reasonable.

Put her in the crate after a strenuous romp with her new family. When you take her out of the crate, carry her where you want her to relieve herself. Stand by quietly pretending to ignore her so she will get down to business. When it is accomplished, as advised above, praise her lavishly! If you keep your dog crated longer than two hours, be sure to keep fresh drinking water in her crate. It is not fair to limit water in order to decrease urine volume. Common sense and any veterinarian will tell you this is asking for health problems.

Provided it is used properly, a crate has many uses, including as a positive housetraining aid.

Sleeping Arrangements

Many experts suggest that if you crate your new dog at night, that you should move the crate into your bedroom, for the obvious reason that dogs are social pack animals. If you have other established pets who sleep in another sleeping area, it will also be suitable for the new kid to "den up" with them, whenever she is old enough, or is accepted by them.

In the beginning, you will need to set your alarm halfway through the night and take her to her potty place. (It doesn't matter how tired you are, don't move her potty area to your bedroom!) If you are taking a young puppy to bed with you, you will be surprised how quickly she will be able to "make it all night."

You also need to put pillows around your bed on the floor in the event that she decides to take the proverbial flying leap. I have found that when allowing them in bed, most puppies by age 4½ months are sleeping through the night and have never wished to leave the bed at night (or in the morning either, for that matter!).

If your new Griffon is your only animal and she will be sleeping away from you in her own area of the house, make sure her bed is cozy, warm and comfortable. Provide a large stuffed animal for her to rest her chin on, and perhaps a ticking clock or sound machine with ocean waves or a simulated heartbeat.

You may prefer to provide your Brussels Griffon puppy with a soft bed for your home and save the crate for any required traveling.

Griff-Proof Your Yard

When you first go out to check every inch of the perimeter of your fenced yard, pretend you are the size of a tiny Griffon puppy and then look for escape routes only *half* that size. Griffons can wiggle through gates, under fences or out of any hole you are sure is too tiny for them. Why do they want out? Beats me! They hear children playing next door, they stand in the center of the yard, look up and see squirrels in the neighbor's trees, they hear your voice on the other side talking with a neighbor, because the "grass is always greener."

Trust me when I say that your yard is not a place to shut your Griffon into and feel secure that she will stay in it! If it is Griff-proof, your yard is a great place to send her for as long as it takes her to potty and run around for a few minutes. You must check on her frequently and watch her through the windows for the entire length of the outing. Better yet, go outside with her and play a game of fetch after she's done with her business.

Be sure your yard is as safe for your Griffon as the inside of your house.

Anything Can Happen

The catalog of potential mishaps for a pet dog on her own property is enormous. You must be vigilant to any possibility and take as many steps as you can to avert disaster. Never leave home and let your dog have access to the fenced yard through a doggy door, or leave her out while you are gone. She can easily get into trouble and you won't be there to check on her and step in.

If you are putting a new fence in for your Griffon, choose a solid wood fence. They are harder for a dog to climb. The Griff doesn't see as much through it to bark at. People are less likely to molest your dog or try to steal her, and children won't be sticking objects through the fence that could puncture eyes or otherwise injure her. I would suggest pouring concrete under it when you put up the fence.

Electronic Containment Systems

Perhaps these are better than no fence at all, and perhaps not. It all depends on how you use them. It will *not* protect your Griffon from the dangers of other

dogs, children or unwelcome intruders that may enter
your yard. Your Griffon may be chased from her yard
(or she might chase a cat) and will be smart enough
not to want to go through the shock of reentering her
yard. There are more minuses, and of course some
pluses. If you go out into the yard with your Griffon,
these systems are certainly better than no fence at all.
They give your Griff the freedom to run loose and play
with you. You can dig in your flowerbed and not have
to worry about her slipping off unnoticed. (Chances
are she will be digging in the bed right behind you,
uncovering or uprooting your work.) I have friends
who have had these systems laid under their carpet
inside the house to keep some rooms, furniture or outside doorways off limits. I personally think this is quite
a clever, practical idea.

*If you want a
housemate for
your Griffon, it is
wise to consider a
new companion
that is about the
same size.*

A Griffon as a Second Dog

If you already have a beloved pet dog and are planning
to bring another into your home, consider carefully
the personality of the established dog. You must *never*
bring a puppy home and turn her loose with your
established adult dog. Integrating two animals, especially if one is a youngster and the other is established,
is a very touchy business and should be done only
under strict, prolonged supervision. If there is any
question in your mind, do not trust your puppy's life to
the care of the older dog!

A rule of thumb that housemates of opposite sexes usually will not fight (especially if they are spayed and neutered) works most of the time, but there are exceptions. Unless there is a vast difference in size, or the squabble looks serious, it is always best to watch quietly and let them work out the pecking order and their differences. In several weeks, when they are eating near each other and sleeping curled up together, then it would be fairly safe to leave them alone together for short periods and see how they respond. If one of the dogs appears to be browbeaten and unhappy most of the time with her tail down after a month or so, it is probable that the personalities are not working together.

If your other dog is considerably larger than the Griffon, please be very careful. Young Griffons should *never* be left unsupervised with any large dog. A large breed *puppy* should never be permitted to play with a Griffon of any age.

Griffon temperament often shows a good deal of terrier influence, and it is not unusual for a Griffon to aggressively confront another dog with a considerable show of growling and bluster. This is their way of telling other dogs that they are tough and "don't even *try* to push me around!" They must get this fact established with other dogs because considering their small size, they would be at a disadvantage if it ever came to a real dispute.

Another Animal Friend?

It is especially important to consider a friend for your new Brussels Griffon if she will be left alone for long periods of time.

Another dog, or even a cat, will usually fit the bill. If you work and your puppy has now grown into an older teen, where she can spend more time at home while you are gone, or if you are acquiring an older teen or a cat-friendly adult, you may want to get your Griffon a kitten. The kitten should have been raised around dogs and be declawed, spayed or neutered, and have her shots up to date. The kitten must be able to get away from the dog and watch from a safe distance until they bond. If a kitten isn't in the cards, another dog will make a wonderful companion with which to wile away some lonely hours until you return home.

If you are crazy about Griffons, you may be thinking about two. This usually happens to a Griffon owner, sooner or later, and it can be a wonderful situation. I would not, however, suggest that you purchase two puppies at once, or littermates. Also, please *never* get a male and a female with the idea of breeding them and recovering your purchase price.

Two puppies will detract from each individual's "quality time with you," create unnecessary jealousy and the puppies will bond with each other rather than with you. You will never have quite the relationship you need with either individual. It is better to wait until the first Griffon is established in your home and is comfortable with your routine before getting the second. If you feel that you really must have two right now, you might seek a congenial adult at the time you get a puppy.

Two Griffons are well-matched company for each other and twice the fun for you.

The best situation would be to acquire the mother, which may have been spayed during a cesarean section, or a spayed adult nanny to your puppy from the same breeder. The breeder will know which of the Griffons will truly be an asset to the puppy's development and not have a hidden mean streak or turn on the little one in your absence.

The Good Traveler

Your Griffon will be ready to go wherever you go. The safest place for her in a car is in a crate with a belt around it, just as the safest place for you is in your seatbelt. If you insist on letting your Griffon ride loose in the car, please *do not* let her put her head out of the window. Her eyes can easily be injured by insects or debris, and she can also jump out. I have seen this happen at a traffic light, so please don't take a chance on it! Also be sure someone has a good grip on her each and every time the car door is opened.

Allowing your dog freedom in a moving car is terribly dangerous and it could easily be fatal under a host of circumstances. Be sure the weather permits comfort for your little lady if you leave her alone in the car for a few minutes (see Chapter 7, "Keeping Your Brussels Griffon Healthy"). If the weather is too warm or too cold, she is better off at home, regardless of what she

If you accustom your Griffon to a traveling crate or carrier as a puppy, she will always be a pleasure to take anywhere.

thinks! Do not leave your car window rolled down far enough for anyone to get their hand in. Whenever you travel with your Griffon, take a margarine tub full of water and tuck it under your seat.

Griffons are great air travelers, too. For a nominal fee, they can travel right under your seat in a soft carrier. Be sure you have a little container for water, a couple of dog biscuits or kibble if the flight is very long, a leash, a couple of paper towels and some plastic baggies, a piece of rawhide or favorite toy or newspaper to put down in the airplane bathroom if the puppy gets restless and needs to potty. Soon she will be a seasoned traveler!

chapter 5

Feeding Your
Brussels Griffon

"You are what you eat" applies as much to dogs as to ourselves. One of the most important ways you can do the best for your beloved Brussels Griffon is to feed him a high-quality brand of dry kibble dog food purchased at a feed store or other store that has a quick turnover so the food you buy will be fresh. This will need no supplementation to be a complete and balanced diet. Your pet should always have a bowl of fresh water available, always in the same place. His nutritional requirements will change with his age, as do ours, so a Brussels Griffon puppy should eat food designed for puppies for about two and a half years. Adult food should be fed from 2½ years to 7 or 8 years of age, and after that you should feed food designed for seniors.

Canned Food or Dry Kibble

I prefer to feed only dry kibble for many reasons. It can be left out without spoiling. It provides gum and tooth exercise that dogs need. It doesn't stick as easily to the gums or teeth, causing premature gum disease; therefore, my dogs' teeth will not need early or frequent cleaning. Read the ingredients to select the most natural food, and remember that skin allergies can be caused by food additives and dyes.

A dog will always reflect the quality of his diet in his condition and vitality.

When the kibble is accompanied by a constant supply of fresh water, the healthy dog's own system regulates food and water balance in his body. When a high-quality kibble is fed, the stools produced are healthy, of limited quantity, small in volume and easy to clean up. I've never had a picky eater, and my dogs have always maintained a healthy weight with good muscle tone (though exercise also plays a part in body condition and appetite).

Mealtimes or Free-Feeding

Young puppies require frequent feedings of a high-calorie food. For this reason, I always free-feed dry kibble to puppies to be sure that they get enough calories when they need them. It is not uncommon to see Toy dogs "go limp" from low blood sugar after a strenuous play session (see Chapter 7, "Keeping Your Brussels Griffon Healthy"). Oddly, I have never created a "glutton" by free-feeding. Free-fed puppies usually seem to grow up eating what they need to maintain the proper weight throughout their lives.

There are some dogs that will eat until they explode, and this trait could be genetic, but more often I think it is created by simple greed from "competitive eating" with their littermates. To get proper nutrition, puppies must eat a food designed specifically for them. Kibble is now available for small puppies with small mouths. The advantages of feeding dry kibble has already been noted and it works the same for puppies as for adults. A Griffon puppy of 8 to 12 weeks will have very sharp teeth and needs the chewing exercise that kibble designated for "Puppy, small bite," will provide.

If you feed a Griffon on a fixed schedule, be sure to provide meals at the same time every day.

If you have other dogs, or prefer to feed a traditional mealtime regimen, a young puppy should eat about a quarter of a cup of kibble, four times a day and continue with at least three larger meals a day until he is 8 months old. If a puppy is very young or is weaned too early, he may refuse to eat at first. Rather than trying different types of food, canned food or roast beef, which will spoil his appetite for dry kibble, try sitting on the floor and coaxing him to eat kibble softened with warm water or salt-free bouillon. Play with him and hand him one piece at a time. Children usually love this task. This does take patience, but it usually works because new surroundings and insecurity are the primary reason most puppies won't eat, not the palatability of the actual food.

If you have a newly acquired adult, be sure to continue him on the kibble he was eating, slowly mixing in your own. Adults can do with one feeding a day, but I prefer to also give them a small breakfast. If he is refusing to eat, watch him carefully to be sure that he is not ill. Monitor his water intake, as he *must* drink plenty of fresh water.

A healthy adult will not hold out for goodies long enough to starve, and he should be provided fresh food at the same time, in a quiet place, each day. Leave the food down for twenty minutes. If you feel there is a health problem, talk with your vet, otherwise do not give in and ply him with gourmet snacks or you will reinforce his hunger strike. If you are free-feeding dry kibble and your adult doesn't appear to be eating, be persistent. Soon you will hear him crunching away.

Be sure your Griffon's food dish is comfortable for him to use. This becomes an important matter with short-faced dogs.

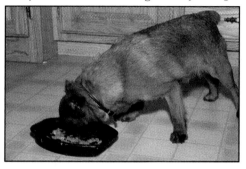

SUPPLEMENTAL FEEDING

If you *never* feed your dog at the table, he will never beg at mealtime. If *anyone* does this just once, your bright little Griffon will forever be watching the table.

Not only will you have created a nuisance at mealtimes, this *supplementing* can also make him a picky eater and rob him of the precious balanced nutrients of his dog food. A high-quality brand of dog food will be nutritionally complete and only need supplements if prescribed by your vet. People often upset this delicate balance in dog food by imposing their own ideas of feeding on their dogs. If you feel you must feed something extra, please use common sense.

A very young puppy that has been weaned too early or that is immature might enjoy a breakfast of plain yogurt. Later, this can be mixed with some pieces of small-bite puppy kibble. Cottage cheese is a favorite food for puppies, or

TO SUPPLEMENT OR NOT TO SUPPLEMENT?

If you're feeding your dog a diet that's correct for her developmental stage and she's alert, healthy looking and neither over-nor underweight, you don't need to add supplements. These include table scraps as well as vitamins and minerals. In fact, a growing puppy is in danger of developing musculoskeletal disorders by over-supplementation. If you have any concerns about the nutritional quality of the food you're feeding, discuss them with your veterinarian.

perhaps a breakfast supplement for an adult. If you can start your puppy eating plain, unsweetened yogurt instead of cottage cheese, it will provide more calcium plus give him the healthy intestinal bacteria all animals and people need. A poached egg is another good food to mix with some kibble for breakfast. Both the egg and the yogurt can be completely mixed in the kibble, whereas canned food and table scraps will not coat the kibble and your Griffon is likely to pick out pieces of meat and leave the kibble behind.

Treats

The first misconception about treats is that the dog knows how big they are. Dogs mainly use their sense of smell and then they gulp food down. They might know how many times they smell something, but they aren't watching to see if a rival got a bigger piece than they did. Treats do not have to be big! Treats can be very small pieces of cheese, dog biscuit or vegetables.

If, like this young owner, you enjoy giving your dog treats, be sure not to overdo them. Treats should be used as training aids or rewards for good behavior, not replacements for the dog's regular diet.

Often, great treats are simply a piece of kibble of a different brand than the dog is eating for its regular meals. Another treat that our Griffons love are bagged baby carrots. Although when feeding them it is always necessary to stand by in case of choking as Griffons don't usually chew their food thoroughly. Anytime treats become commonplace or filling, you are in danger of putting the dog off his balanced meals or starting a *hunger strike.*

Dangerous Foods

Common sense must prevail here, and care must be taken to keep any tasty items that a Griffon could possibly get into out of the trash. Chops, fish, poultry and most beef bones are a definite *No.* Put lids on empty jars before throwing them out so that your Griffon doesn't stick his head into the jar. Foil of any kind is dangerous. Foil smelling of food or chocolate will be very enticing. Chocolate alone can kill your dog, so please watch children and keep candy dishes covered and up high. Cat food should be kept away from your Griffon. While it isn't instantly lethal, steady snacks of cat food can cause major health problems for your dog.

Possibly the most important warning of all—please DO NOT allow your pet to become obese! Nothing will shorten his life or stress his joints more quickly. If you are having a problem with obesity, you are probably "supplementing" your Griffon's diet. Cut him back to strictly dry kibble only. If this doesn't work, have him checked over by your vet for any disorder. If he is healthy, buy a kibble for overweight dogs and feed just the amount suggested by your vet. Overweight adults can have salt-free canned green beans mixed into their dry kibble. This provides bulk in the stomach, while adding no calories.

If your vet determines that your Griffon has a health problem, dog food companies make a variety of special diets for special health needs. Ask your vet and be guided by his or her suggestions.

chapter 6

Grooming Your
Brussels Griffon

Often when an individual or a family is "smitten" by a breed of dog, the question, "How much grooming is involved," is one of the first to be asked. Quite properly, prospective new owners wonder how much shedding can be expected, and how having this dog in the home will add to the workload of the vacuum and to housekeeping routines in general. As you will discover in this chapter, maintaining a happy, healthy Brussels Griffon goes far beyond running your vacuum cleaner.

Grooming in Show or Pet Styles

If you are interested in showing your Griffon, there is little difference in grooming procedures for the smooth Griffon pet or show dog. However, the rough Griffon that will be shown must be "hand-stripped." The harshness of the rough coat is a very important feature in the show ring, and to keep it harsh, it must be plucked out with finger and thumb. Pulling out the Griffon's hair is time-consuming and requires practice and patience. Stripping or plucking are only required, however, if a Griffon is to be shown.

Some owners like the look of a hand-stripped coat, even if they are not planning to show. If you decide to have your Griffon trimmed in this manner, it is best for you to hire an experienced groomer to strip your dog. You should be ready to pay much more than if you had her pet-clipped. Also, if you have her clipped, she may shed a little more, her coat will become a little softer-textured and lighter in color.

If you purchased your Griffon to show, go to the breeder and either learn how to strip the coat yourself (as this is an ongoing process that must be started when the puppy is quite young), or find out where you should take your dog for this process. If you plan to have your rough Griffon clipped, she will look very cute in a modified Schnauzer trim, without the eyebrows. If the weather is a little chilly, remember to always have a coat or sweater handy for the smooth, or the rough after stripping or a short clip!

The use of a flea comb, as illustrated here, is essential in grooming either a smooth or a rough Griffon. There are several models to choose from, so ask your dog's breeder for suggestions.

Grooming Tools

Every Griffon needs attention every day to her personal hygiene as surely as you and I do. When caring day to day for the rough coat, in my opinion, the most important grooming tools you can have are your fingers and a good steel, fine-toothed flea comb with rounded teeth. These can usually be ordered from any of the kennel supply mail order catalogs; the price is usually under ten dollars. Do not buy a comb with plastic teeth or sharp-pointed teeth.

You will also need a pair of long-bladed, sharp barber's scissors, preferably with blunt tips. You will also need a good sharp pair of dog nail clippers or scissors and some styptic powder. If you can find them, I recommend that you buy the scissors-type, rather than the guillotine nail clippers. For cleaning the rough coat between baths, you will need corn starch and a pin brush or a waterless shampoo.

Daily Grooming

The smooth may only need her face wiped with a tissue dampened in baby oil. The rough should have the inside corners of her eyes carefully combed each day with a flea comb to remove "sleepers" (collected matter). If your Griffon has folds over her nose or under her eyes, or a deep stop (the space between the eyes), then these areas should be cleaned daily with tissue and baby oil. Water should never be used in crevices or folds because it encourages the growth of fungus.

You will benefit along with your Griffon by paying regular attention to her face and teeth.

Dogs of both coat types should get a thorough combing with the flea comb. Not only will you and your Griffon really enjoy this time, but it will give you a chance to remove dead hairs and alert you to the unwelcome presence of a flea or tick picked up during a walk. After a complete combing, if you wish to brush your dog, you may, but it isn't necessary.

During this daily grooming session, accustom your Griffon to having your fingers in her mouth. Wrap a small piece of gauze over your finger and gently rub the teeth and gums. You must be sensitive to the fact that lifting the lips of this flat-faced breed may close off her nostrils, and she could panic. Take special care with this, especially when checking her top front teeth.

If your puppy has retained any baby canine teeth (see "Weekly Grooming," below), part of her daily oral care will involve putting the gauze over your thumbnail and gently pushing any foreign matter from between these teeth until your vet removes those that don't come out on their own.

Weekly Grooming

At least once every week, you must add extras to your daily grooming session. Check the nails to make sure they have not grown too long. As a Griffon's nails are black, shortening them is literally and figuratively a stab in the dark, but a necessary one.

Make a visual inspection of the teeth along with the gauze rub. Brussels Griffon puppies often retain their baby canine teeth (four fangs, two top and two bottom). When the adult canine teeth come in beside the baby teeth, there will be "double fangs" with a very tight spot between them where food, hair and foreign matter can lodge. This accumulation will soon begin to decay and cause mouth odor.

If unattended, tooth decay and worse will eventually result. The situation will lead to gum disease, which can spiral down to systemic infection through the entire body. These baby teeth will need to be removed by your vet. While I do not have my Griffons anesthetized more often than necessary, I try to keep retained teeth clean until the dog is spayed or neutered (or perhaps cropped) so any procedures requiring anesthesia can all be done at the same time.

If your Griffon is rough-coated, you will need to keep hair pulled from the inside corner of each eye. The hair should not be allowed to grow here as it will irritate the

The rough Griffon will need regular attention to keep her face hair from irritating the eyes.

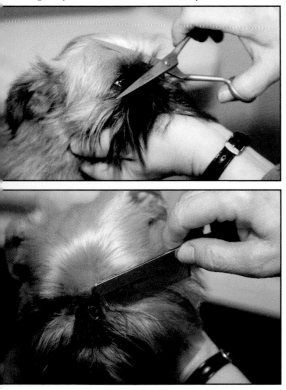

The flea comb is the idea tool for combing the whiskers on a rough Griffon.

eye. It is much easier for you and safer for your dog if you get in the habit of keeping the hair pulled rather than trying to trim it with scissors.

First comb the hair with the flea comb, then firmly grasp the little hairs at the inside corner of each eye and pull them out in the direction of their normal growth, *just a few at a time.* There will be a struggle at first, but your Griffon will eventually learn to tolerate this fetish of yours with a measure of resignation. The hairs comes out quite easily as long as you don't take too many at once, and this is really necessary for your dog's health. When I pull the hair at the corners of the eyes, I also pull the hair out from the stop. The hair in the stop will grow long and curl down the nosepad into the nostrils. This can be trimmed flat above the nose by laying a long, sharp pair of scissors along the top of the nosepad.

I find it is easier and safer for the dog to pull out this long hair. When trimming this area, I use a LONG pair of scissors so that the ends (whether pointed or blunt) are far away from the eyes, and out to the side of the face. Here I cut with the center of the scissors flat by the dog's nose.

Once a week I also check the hair around the anus, vulva or sheath of the penis to see if it needs trimming. The hair around your Griffon's eyes, nose and genitals may not need weekly trimming, but if you check it and keep it trimmed as needed, it will stretch the interval between professional trims and keep your dog healthier and nicer to be near.

Use a good ear cleaner once a week, and after waiting the directed time, gently wipe the cleaner and dirt from the ears with cotton swabs, being careful not to go too far into the ear. I always give my dogs' ears the "sniff test" before cleaning them. A foul-smelling ear means an infection or parasite infestation, and your Griffon needs prompt veterinary attention before a problem develops. Healthy ears will smell very little, and the smell certainly won't be offensive.

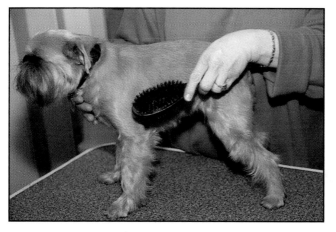

A quality brush is essential in keeping a Griffon's coat and skin healthy, regardless of coat type.

Flea Control with a Flea Comb

If you suspect your Griffon may have fleas, keep a small bowl of water with dish soap in it handy while you comb her. Work in a brightly lit area, and if you need glasses, wear them. Fleas are *very fast* and they can jump about a yard. If you lose one, you will never see it again. Have several layers of white paper towels beside you.

After each combing, quickly check the comb and remove the hair to the paper towel and look through the hair again. If you see something moving on the comb, hold it under water while you pull the hair out of the comb. Fleas hate water and will drown easily. Be sure they don't climb up the hair and hop out of the water. You cannot kill fleas by squeezing them between your fingers. Fleas are flat and hard-shelled. You must crack them between the backs of your nails if you don't want to drown them.

Continue to comb your dog over and over, even in those places you have already combed until you are convinced that you have them all. If you comb daily and have just found a flea or two, you should be okay. If you haven't combed for a while and you have found several fleas and flea dirt (black grit in the hair, usually above the dog's tail), you will need to de-flea your home, yard, etc (see Chapter 7, "Keeping Your Brussels Griffon Healthy") and oil your dog using the directions that follow.

Putting Your Dog "In Oil"

Parasites suffocate in oil. Although oiling your Griffon is messy, you will be completely free from worry about the adverse reactions of using chemicals on her skin to fight parasites. I use a generic bath oil because it seems more water-soluble than baby oil, which easily works as well. Stand your dog in a sink with the plug in place. Mix the oil with equal parts of warm water. Saturate her starting at the neck. Comb the solution through her hair to the skin with the flea comb. Be sure to lightly comb the solution into the hair on her head and ears. Don't forget legs, underarms, belly and groin area.

If the parasite you seek to eliminate is cheyletiella, you may also apply undiluted oil along the spine and comb it through. Keep cleaning the off-white substance, which will be the mites and debris, from your flea comb onto a paper towel. Continue this for at least ten minutes or until the skin looks clean. For cheyletiella, repeat this in a week and then wait two weeks and give one more oil bath to be sure reinfestation is less likely.

This type of oil can easily be washed from the hair after a couple of hours, or if left on, it will disappear in a few days. Either way, it improves the skin and smells pleasant. Blot your Griffon with a towel, but do not thoroughly dry her for an hour or so. Keep her in a very warm place because the oiled hair will not insulate her from cold. She may develop a slightly loose stool from licking some oil off her feet or from oil that comes off her whiskers into the water bowl, but this should not be a problem and is far less a potential health hazard than the use of chemical pesticides.

Bathing

Brussels Griffons are naturally very clean and tidy little dogs and should be bathed only when really necessary. The smooth-coated variety will require much less attention to grooming than his bewhiskered, rough-coated brother. However, do remember that a very close ancestor of the Brussels Griffon is the Affenpinscher-type

Give your Griffon a bath only when necessary, taking every precaution for safety.

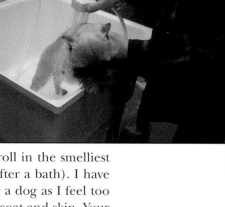

or the stable ratter, and these were very game, feral, busy little guys with all of their natural instincts intact and operating full tilt.

Those early traits are now somewhat diluted by the influence of the other breeds of origin, but it is not uncommon to find the Griffon who thinks her life's work is to catch mice or roll in the smelliest element she can find (always just after a bath). I have never believed in routinely bathing a dog as I feel too many baths will dry out a Griffon's coat and skin. Your sense of smell or touch will usually tell you when it is bath time.

Baths are an important part of grooming and should only be given by someone who is thoroughly familiar with Griffons in general and the dog to be bathed in particular. Under no circumstances should this care essential be left to children unless they are carefully taught and very responsible. Skin irritation can result from soap that is not thoroughly removed, and a puppy can easily become frightened by the experience.

Griffons are usually not thrilled with baths. They become virtual role models of resistance, and their paws become like little hands enabling your Griffon to climb right up your arms and hang on like a monkey. A soft towel folded in the bottom of a sink equipped with a sprayer and having your body close will help your dog's sense of security, but *do* be prepared to get a little wet yourself.

I put a drop of pure mineral oil, from a clean dropper and container that I have filled just for eyes, into each eye. I also drop mineral oil into each ear canal from a different container. This seems to offer some protection to the eyes in the event some soap runs that way. It also helps keep water from the ears while rinsing.

If fleas are a problem, wet a circle around the entire neck (fleas will not cross water) before wetting the rest of the dog. As I mentioned in the previous section, I prefer to use no chemicals on my dogs. Buy a good shampoo specifically designed for a dog's skin from your vet or pet store. I lather my Griff the first time to get the dirt off, and at the same time I check the anal glands and express them if they need it. Use your fingertips to massage the body and skin and loosen dead hair. Your little friend will love this and it will help her relax. Rinse her and then suds her again. During this sudsing, I start at the top of the neck between the ears and comb to the skin with a flea comb.

This is a slow process with the rough coat, but it is worth it. I comb through to the skin along the entire coat, my other hand holding the skin above the comb as I go along. Doing this will keep you familiar with her skin and help you to notice any irritation, new lumps or developing skin tumors that should be looked at by your vet. You will stop often to clean the hair from the comb. Lay the hair on a paper towel beside you, and as you work you can scan it for fleas (they will be dead by now, but you should be aware if your dog had them). The flea comb will remove a tremendous amount of dead hair, and you will know that you have thoroughly cleaned your pet.

Rinse the entire dog carefully and completely, again starting with the neck and working down from there.

Do not forget under the armpits and the tummy, genitals and under the chin. Soap scum left on your Griffon's skin will cause flakes and itching. Last, I wipe the face clean with a washcloth. I also use a cotton swab to clean the oil, along with any dirt, from the ears. Finally, as with daily grooming, I again use the trusty flea comb in the corners of the eyes.

Drying After a Bath

This is playtime for my dogs if I have bathed several. After blotting them with towels between some good shakes, I then sit on the floor with them and some dry towels. I throw a towel over each dog and rub it with both hands, especially around the neck, and talk to them in what I call my "play voice." I let them tear around the house for a moment, calling them back for another rub with another dry towel, which they dearly love. This activity warms them up and gets their blood flowing, relaxes them after a stressful time in the sink and gives them something to look forward to.

Towel-dry your Griffon right after the bath and, if you wish, use a hand-held hair dryer to finish. Be sure to keep your Griffon indoors and out of drafts for several hours after bathing.

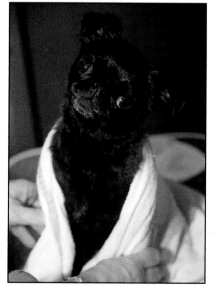

If you decide to do this, you'll find it's fun for you, too! Be sure to pay special attention to the areas around your Griffon's neck and above the tail to lessen the danger of hot spots. You might want to dry your Griffon extra carefully here. If you prefer to use a hair dryer, be sure it is on the warm setting, and rub the coat with a towel, or comb the hair in the direction of natural growth as you dry it.

CLEANING THE COAT BETWEEN BATHS

After a muddy walk on the street or a romp in the woods, you will want to clean your Griff before turning her loose on your carpet. If you have been walking on winter-salted sidewalks, be sure to wash the salt from her feet.

To clean soil from the coat, lay her on a towel and blot the moisture from her coat. Rub or brush corn starch or talc through the belly and leg hair and allow it to dry. Brush the powder out and you will be surprised how clean your Griff will be. If you prefer, you can also purchase waterless shampoos for dogs that you can rub in, towel off and then dry your dog as usual.

Anal Glands

Do be careful who you trust to squeeze your dog's anal sacs. I think that most of the trouble with ruptured or infected anal glands were started by someone who thought they knew what they were doing but squeezed them improperly and too often. This is not a task for just anyone, simply because they think they can do it.

Often squeezing the anal sacs is done by a groomer who is in too much of a hurry and is not careful enough to express them from *behind* the gland. This forces some of the contents backwards which can irritate or rupture the gland. A ruptured gland will soon be evident, but a repeatedly and too-frequently irritated gland will end up infected.

Talk to your vet about the possibility of loss of bowel control (often when the dog barks), if surgery to remove the glands is suggested because of chronic infection or rupture. Better yet, try to prevent any problems in the first place. Ask your vet to teach you how to express the sacs yourself. In this way, you can feel them with light pressure to see if they are full, rather than expressing them in a routine fashion more often than needed.

Nail Trimming

As mentioned earlier in this chapter, maintaining short nails is vital to the health and well being of your Griffon. Imagine how you would feel if you always wore ill-fitting shoes. Long nails cause damage and later arthritis to the joints and toes. A nail can curl around and grow into the foot pad. A long or split nail can get caught in something and be torn or pulled out, causing profuse bleeding and tremendous pain.

I know you will feel bad if you draw a little blood when clipping the nails, but this is far better for your dog than if you let the nails grow long so that each step causes pain. If you cut a little every week, the vein carrying the blood supply (the quick) will recede and keeping the nails short will become very easy.

Be sure to check both the pasterns (wrists) and the rear feet for retained or grown back dewclaws. The nail on these can curl right around and grow back into the leg. Dewclaws, which are analogous to our thumbs, usually have a very small blood supply enabling these nails to be clipped almost right to the leg. Keep a container of styptic power open and close by whenever you trim nails. In that way, if you do get into a quick, you can hold a pinch of powder to the end of the nail until the bleeding stops. If you are unable to clip the nails yourself, you must have your vet or groomer do it at least once a month.

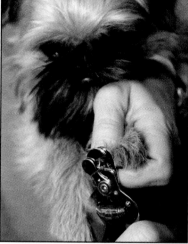

Weekly attention to a Griffon's nails will keep them from growing too long.

71

chapter 7

Keeping Your
Brussels Griffon
Healthy

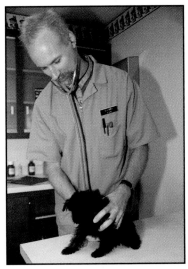

Finding the Right Veterinarian

Owning and caring for a dog is expensive, and if you aren't willing or able to do it properly, please don't even start. Even before you bring your new Brussels Griffon home, you must interview and select a veterinarian. Select one that inspires your confidence and trust. Never make your selection based on fees for services or location. The least (or most) expensive or the closest may not be the best. If you must drive across town for the best and safest surgery, it is not too far; however, try to also locate an emergency clinic in your own area. A good way to find a veterinarian who has expertise in brachycephalic breeds is to call your local kennel club. Dogs having flat faces also have greater sensitivity to anesthesia and a greater likelihood of breathing disorders, so the veterinarian you settle on should be aware of this. Most medium-sized and large cities will have at least one kennel club and the telephone number is usually listed, or it would be available through the American Kennel Club (AKC).

Often the local kennel club will also run ads in the newspaper to help people find reputable breeders and educate the public. Once you have the number of your local kennel club, ask for the numbers of local breeders of other brachycephalic breeds. The breeders of Bulldogs or Pekingese are among the first I would ask a referral from.

Breeders that show their dogs make it their business to know everything possible about health care, they have more experience with surgery and they have usually found a vet that they can have a "give-and-take" relationship with. Often, the pet owner is too intimidated by their veterinarian's knowledge to remember the questions he or she needs to ask or to relate pertinent diagnostic facts to help determine the problem. The vet is only able to diagnose a condition based on a few minutes spent examining the animal and on what the owner is able to report. Show dog breeders have used veterinary services extensively; they have spent hours or days deciphering problems and have sought a vet who will take their impressions of the problem into serious consideration. This is the type of veterinarian you want to form a relationship of trust with.

Vaccinations

When I let a puppy go to his new home, his shots are current and he has usually had three. In this way, his immunity to distemper, hepatitis and parvovirus is built up gradually. A baby's first immunity comes from his mother's colostrum or first milk. This immunity can last for several months, but it is hard to tell for sure just when it wears off and leaves the puppy unprotected. This is why shots are given at about three-week intervals, to protect the puppy as the mother's natural immunity wears off. If a shot is given during the period of natural immunity, it does no good and the puppy is unprotected when the natural immunity does wear off. Some puppies have still had natural immunity to *parvovirus* at 19 weeks of age, so I am always sure to get the last parvo shot after the puppy is 20 weeks old.

Your Griffon's vaccinations at all life stages are among his most important health safeguards.

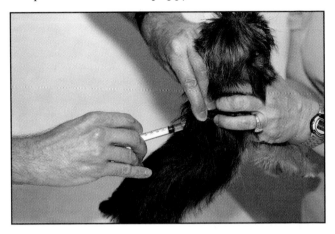

Each veterinarian has his or her own way of scheduling shots and I believe if you have carefully selected your vet, then you need to follow his/her advice on inoculation schedules and types. Your vet will know, perhaps better than the breeder living in another area of the country, what diseases are prevalent where you live. Current research is being done regarding frequency and types of vaccinations and also reactions to the leptospirosis vaccine, so be sure to choose a vet who stays abreast of this and other current issues. The standard diseases that dogs are vaccinated against include:

Distemper is a highly contagious viral disease. It is an airborne infection harbored by raccoons and other wild animals along with unvaccinated neighboring dogs. Symptoms include high fever, cough, vomiting, diarrhea and seizures. Symptoms continue to get worse and usually lead to death.

Canine hepatitis is a contagious viral disease that affects the liver. The first sign is often red eyes and a mucous discharge, followed by fever, abdominal pain, vomiting and diarrhea, then death.

Leptospirosis is a bacterial disease spread by the urine of wild carriers or infected animals. Due to the high population of mice and rats carrying leptospirosis, it is a good idea to discuss this with your vet. Toy dogs are more susceptible to vaccine reactions, and leptospirosis vaccine is currently a controversial issue. If you do decide to vaccinate for lepto, plan to stay at the vet's office for a half hour after the shot is given in case your Griffon develops an allergic reaction. Hold your dog on your lap while you read a good book. The time will pass quickly enough, and if your dog gets into trouble, the vet is right there.

Parainfluenza or "kennel cough" is a very contagious upper respiratory infection. The first sign is a dry, nonproductive, hacking cough.

Bordatella is another strain of kennel cough. It is also highly contagious, but there is more fluid in the nostrils. It can quickly lead to pneumonia and become fatal in puppies, weakened adults or seniors.

Parvovirus and *coronavirus* are both viral diseases. Dogs become lethargic and develop high fever with bloody diarrhea. Death usually follows rapidly.

Rabies is a virus transmitted through the saliva of infected animals. This vaccine is required

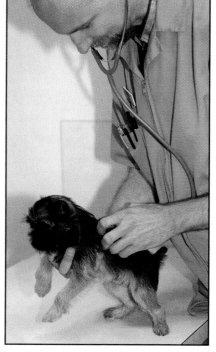

It is essential to have a new puppy examined by the veterinarian as soon as possible after you bring him home.

by state law for every dog. In many communities, you will need a certificate from your vet to get your annual dog license. Once the symptoms appear, there is no known cure for rabies and the disease is always fatal. Unless your state requires rabies vaccination for dogs younger than 6 months of age, or you live in a high-risk situation, wait until your Griffon is 6 months old before getting him this inoculation.

Fortunately, highly effective immunizations are available against these diseases. Inoculate your Griffon on schedule. Don't walk him where many other dogs relieve themselves, and keep him away from sickly looking animals. When you bring your Griffon to the vet, bring him in a carrier; don't take him out and don't let anyone else in the waiting room come near him. Take your own towel to the vet's office for the table and don't put your Griffon on the floor at any time. If he becomes ill, get him to your vet quickly. Your vet can diagnose the problem. Many of these diseases have similar symptoms but will be treated differently.

SENSITIVITY TO VACCINES

Anaphylaxis (allergic shock) is not common; I've had two cases in thirty years. But it is common enough to warrant mention. Dogs known to react to their shots should be given an antihistamine a couple of hours beforehand, and still be watched closely by the vet. Dogs usually react within a half hour after the shot, but the one of mine that reacted waited almost three hours after the shot and then his face blew up like a balloon. His lips and throat thickened. I gave him a shot of epinephrine, and by the time I got him to the vet, he was fine. Some dogs get better on their own, some die. Allergic shock demands immediate attention. If shots are given at home, do so only when your vet has business hours.

BOOSTER SHOTS

When the series of puppy shots is complete, a booster shot will then be needed annually. This is also a good time for the yearly physical and fecal check. If it is in early spring, you can combine this visit with the annual heartworm check. It is vitally important not to let the date for the annual booster shots slide by and be forgotten.

Thermometers

Keep a thermometer handy for your Griffon. Always take his temperature rectally. A dog's normal temperature is in a range of about 101.5°F to 102.5°F. The thermometer is the first thing you should reach for if you think your dog does not feel well. If you are using a glass thermometer, continue *to hold it* in place for the full three minutes. One of my dogs drew the thermometer inside and it was a full day of constant supervision until it could be retrieved!

Internal Parasites

Your puppy should be free of worms and protozoans when you bring him home, but you should take a stool sample along for his first visit to his vet, just in case something was missed. Some breeders will worm their puppies on their own, without first confirming the type of worm or even if no worms are present. This can result in unnecessary toxins being introduced into the puppy's system, the wrong wormer used or protozoans missed in self-diagnosis. Worms and protozoans can be devastating for a dog; however, *for a puppy they can be fatal!* Do not put off taking a stool sample to your vet if you think your dog may have any kind of internal parasites.

More than likely your dog will pick up worms or protozoans occasionally while visiting the park or other public places people generally walk their dogs. This is another good reason to always take a stool sample along for your Griffon's annual check up. Ask your vet to be sure to also check for protozoans. Protozoans require a different lens and higher microscopic magnification to be diagnosed than worm eggs, and different treatment.

Roundworms are probably the most common worms that plague dogs and their owners and your puppy can be born with them. The roundworm-infested puppy might look unthrifty with a distended belly and dull coat. Or you may just see one or more live worms, resembling spaghetti, passed in the stool.

Hookworms can be extremely hard to get rid of, both in your dog and in your yard. These nasty worms can lead to severe blood loss and anemia. Hookworms are also passed through the mother's milk, so if your dog or your property has a history of hookworms, worm early and repeatedly along with a strict disinfecting schedule of the environment. Follow-up fecal checks should be done for months after you think your Griffon is negative.

Whipworm is also very difficult to get rid of and can do a lot of damage to your Griffon. Because whipworms only shed their eggs periodically, it also may not show up on the first stool check. In fact, you may need four or five fecal checks before confirming whipworms. You will need to be strict about sanitation both indoors and out and do follow-up fecal checks.

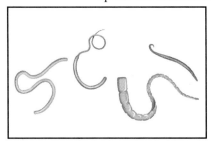

Common internal parasites (l-r): roundworm, whipworm, tapeworm and hookworm.

Tapeworm is the second most common worm and almost always follows a flea infestation. The dog's coat may appear dry or brittle. Tapeworm segments may be found in the dog's stool or stuck in the hair around the anus, appearing as small white grains of rice. Tapeworm eggs do not always show up in a fecal test, even though the dog is known to be infected.

Heartworm infestation is far easier to prevent than to treat. The treatment can be risky and has killed many infected dogs. It is very important to talk with your vet about blood tests and preventative treatment. Heartworm can be passed to your dog through the bite of an infected mosquito and can only be detected by a blood test.

Protozoans   The most common protozoans in dogs are coccidia and giardia. These are tiny, single-celled organisms and can infect your dog through drinking water, or your dog licking his feet after a walk in an infested area. Coccidia generally persists in a kennel with poor sanitation and cramped quarters. Both can occur with intermittent bouts of bloody diarrhea and both may not always show up on a fecal exam. Puppies are particularly susceptible. Once diagnosed, both are treatable by your vet. Suspect protozoans if your dog passes slimy diarrhea or shows sporadic mucous or blood in his stool.

External Parasites

Fleas are likely to become a problem at some point during the life of your dog, and will need attention for his continued health. An occasional flea picked up during a walk can be taken care of easily during the dog's daily flea combing. If you follow the directions in "Flea Control with a Flea Comb," described in chapter 6, you will be aware that you have a flea or two and get a *jump* ahead of them before they infest your house and yard. If you are facing a heavier flea infestation, use an oil rinse as described in chapter 6, and use flea products suggested by your vet for your house, bedding and yard. If you *do* use flea products on your dog, your vet will know which are compatible with those used in your home environment. Certain chemicals *must not* be used together and, in combination, can kill your pet.

The flea is a die-hard pest.

Your Brussels Griffons will share your home, and so the need to keep them parasite-free speaks for itself.

Cheyletiella (walking dandruff) can be a problem in areas with heavy squirrel or rabbit populations. It is also carried on other dogs or cats. You may not know you have a problem until your own arms and abdomen break out and itch. Unfortunately, these little mites thrive on puppies, though adult dogs can become infested as well. Just like people, some dogs seem not to notice them and others scratch themselves silly. An affected dog's skin will have off-white or yellow patches that look like heavy dandruff.

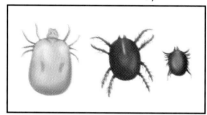
*Three types of
ticks (l-r): the
wood tick,
brown dog tick
and deer tick.*

I have not had success with flea products or insecticides in the control of cheyletiella. Many breeders, myself included, have inadvertently killed darling puppies, trying to rid them of cheyletiella (or fleas) with insecticidal dips and shampoos. *It is not worth the life of your puppy or adult, to rid your dog of any parasite! The cost is permanent! You must keep your focus when you realize that your dog has a parasite infestation!* If your pup has dandruff, dig up the patch with a flea comb. Under the dandruff, you can comb up oval off-white dots, *barely* visible to the eye. Hold your flea comb to the light and if it is warm enough, you will see these tiny dots start to move slowly up and down the teeth of the comb. Or, if you prefer, have your vet confirm this under a microscope.

A chemical called Ivermectin will kill cheyletiella when given as an injection. The chemical will go all through the puppy's system and kill the parasites living on the skin. I would strongly suggest the use of oil first as described in chapter 6. Again this is a nontoxic way to rid your pet of most external parasites, and it really works well on cheyletiella.

Ticks are always a concern and it is simply good sense to check your Griffon carefully after a romp in the woods. You may find a tiny spider-like "hitchhiker" with your flea comb. Often the tick's head

*Use tweezers to
remove ticks
from your dog.*

may be buried in your dog's skin. Prior to laying eggs, females become engorged with blood and can be as large as a pea. The males are always much smaller.

Drip a little alcohol on the tick at the dog's skin to cause it to release its hold. Pull the tick off with tweezers and flush it down the toilet. Apply alcohol to the dog's skin and keep watch over the site for a few days. If it doesn't heal normally, take him to your vet. Most ticks are harmless, but in some areas of the U.S. certain species can carry Rocky Mountain spotted fever and Lyme disease. Ticks can also be a problem in the dog's immediate environment so residences and yards may also need to be treated.

Lyme disease is a serious health problem for both dogs people and certain areas of the United States are hot spots for ticks carrying Lyme disease. Areas heavily inhabited by deer were thought to be the worst, but it is now reported that mice are the most prevalent carriers. If you live in a high risk area, ask your veterinarian about precautions and the vaccination. Griffons are game little dogs. They love to climb or tunnel under the wood pile and hide or root in underbrush where ticks might live. If you live in a high-risk area and your dog appears lame for no reason, he may have contracted Lyme disease and will require immediate attention by your veterinarian.

Keeping Ears Healthy

If your Griffon is continually fussing over his ears, or if you notice a dark accumulation or an unpleasant odor in the ears, you need to take him to the veterinarian as soon as possible. All these signs can indicate ear mite infestation. Fortunately, if you only have one animal, ear mites may be killed by cleaning and dropping mineral oil into the ear canal daily for a month or more. If you have more than one pet or cannot do this with complete consistency, get medication from your vet and use it diligently.

If the problem is not ear mites, a culture should be taken by your vet to insure proper treatment. Ear infections can easily become chronic and you must treat them consistently and long enough with the correct medication.

Mites that cause mange, and *lice* must be diagnosed by your vet, and treated along with the bedding and living quarters with the appropriate insecticides.

Sarcoptic mange is caused by a microscopic mite that burrows under the skin and causes intense itching and hair loss. Sarcoptic mange mites are highly contagious and can also live on humans.

Demodetic mange is caused by a mite that lives in the dog's hair follicles. Stress on the dog seems to be a major contributing factor of the dog developing this form of mange and also of it progressing into *generalized cases*. The demodetic mange mite causes red, then bluish, thickened skin and finally hair loss. Puppies sometimes develop a small, *localized* patch on a front ankle or forehead at 6 or 7 months of age because of the stress puberty puts on their system. This is rarely anything to worry about and it may disappear without treatment. On rare occasions it can turn into a stubborn generalized case and pop up all over the body.

Generalized cases most often occur when the dog is very unhappy and stressed because his needs are not being met properly. He might become an obsessive licker or chewer and develop allergies and neurotic habits along with the generalized mange. Mitaban™ by Upjohn is a highly effective treatment for generalized demodetic mange. It can be toxic to Toy dogs and should be used with care and for a shorter duration than the manufacturer's suggestion. If it is used for *localized* cases, a full dip should never be given. Daubing the properly mixed solution just on the spots, and repeating it two weeks later, will clear it up. However, the skin will look worse before it looks better.

Eye Injuries and Diseases

Most brachycephalic breeds have shallower sockets, thus exposing more of the eyeball than more normally conformed breeds. Combine this larger exposure of the cornea with the absence of a protruding nose to serve as a "bumper," and it becomes easy to understand why these flat-faced breeds are more prone to eye injuries or "dry eye." When a brachycephalic dog bumps into something or receives a blow to his head, the pressure can pop the eyeball from its shallow socket. If this happens, immediately put a wet, clean cloth over the eye (which will be hanging but will still remain attached) and rush him to the emergency vet. If the eye is kept moist and clean, and care is forthcoming, there are usually no problems and sight is not impaired.

Corneal injuries first become noticed when the dog favors an eye or squints. Try to hold the eye open in good light and see if you notice a hole in the cornea. If you see nothing but the dog persists in favoring the eye, go to your vet anyway. If you see nothing and he starts to behave normally, watch him carefully for a few days. If you haven't caught the problem at the start, the cornea will have a light blue or white spot. In extreme cases, the eye will be clamped shut and tear profusely. The dog will hide. Take the dog immediately to an emergency vet. Never put (or allow to be used) eye drops containing a steroid or cortisone into a newly scratched or healing eye! Read the label, sometimes there will be an error when the medicine is dispensed. Steroids can ruin any chance of the eye healing properly.

The healing power of the eye is a marvelous phenomenon! I have seen terrible-looking eyes heal with hardly a scar when treated properly (and constantly). Many eye medications are prescribed as standard three times a day treatment (no doubt for dogs with normally proportioned noses). Brachycephalic breeds will rub their faces on almost everything, especially if an eye is bothering them. This will increase the bacteria in the eye.

IDENTIFY YOUR DOG

It is a terrible thing to think about, but your dog could somehow, someday, get lost or stolen. How would you get him back? Your best bet would be to have some form of identification on your dog. You can choose from a collar and tags, a tattoo, a microchip or a combination of these three.

Every dog should wear a buckle collar with identification tags. They are the quickest and easiest way for a stranger to identify your dog. It's best to inscribe the tags with your name and phone number; you don't need to include your dog's name.

There are two ways to permanently identify your dog. The first is a tattoo, placed on the inside of your dog's thigh. The tattoo should be your social security number or your dog's AKC registration number.

The second is a microchip, a rice-sized pellet that is inserted under the dog's skin at the base of the neck, between the shoulder blades. When a scanner is passed over the dog, it will beep, notifying the person that the dog has a chip. The scanner will then show a code, identifying the dog. Microchips are becoming more and more popular and are certainly the wave of the future.

Ask your vet if putting the medicine in every hour around the clock for the first three days or so, will delay healing. Often the frequency of medication the first few days can make the difference between a healed eye and one requiring surgery and a disappointing outcome. If you feel the eye is healed and discontinue the treatment, you could be mistaken and find the blue spot reappearing, this time to be more stubborn. Do not quit the eye drops until you have had the eye stained and your vet says that it is totally healed.

Dry eye (keratoconjuctivitis sicca) is a problem with many dogs as they age. For some reason they loose the ability to produce tears. This leads to damage of the cornea, pigmentary keratitis and possibly blindness if not treated. Dry eye can be diagnosed by a simple tear test by your vet. There are several methods used to treat this problem that range from dropping artificial tears into the eyes, to the use of a tear stimulant, cyclopsporin. The treatment must be continued for the remainder of the dog's life.

EYELASH ABNORMALITIES

Entropion, distichiasis and trichiasis are abnormalities that cause hair or eyelashes to rub against the cornea. The result is usually pigmentary keratitis and later, often blindness. Surgery is required to correct the problem.

Pigmentary keratitis is a condition where a brown pigmented membrane covers the surface of the cornea due to irritation and rubbing of skin or hair. This is a "protection mechanism," such as a callus on the skin at a point of wear. The key is to catch pigmentary keratitis when you first notice it starting to form. Take your dog to the veterinarian immediately.

CATARACTS

Cataracts can be caused by toxins, nutrition or hereditary factors. They can be located at different sites within the lens. Some become larger, some never do. Cataracts can occur alone or because of other changes in the eye. While cataracts are associated with the geriatric dog, some bloodlines of Brussels Griffons seem to be vulnerable to juvenile cataracts. These are considered hereditary and occur while the dog is young.

Many careful breeders are now getting their breeding stock's eyes certified annually. This is a good subject to discuss with the breeder when you purchase your Griffon.

Respiratory Problems

Stenotic nares can be a problem in Griffons. The openings in the nostrils are not large enough to allow a free flow of air and will restrict breathing. If you pick up and hold your Griffon over your arm, after a little exercise, and he opens his mouth slightly with each breath, check his nostrils. If they pinch in when he tries to inhale, your vet can trim a flap of skin off, (perhaps during an ear crop, spay or the removal of baby canine teeth). You won't believe the "instant difference" this will make in his quality of life. Griffons with this problem should not be used for breeding. Dogs that have had the corrective surgery performed cannot be shown.

Reverse sneezing happens occasionally in dogs with normally proportioned forefaces, but is a common occurrence among flat-faced breeds. It isn't really a health problem, it is just the dog clearing his sinuses. However, the noise he will make and posture he may take could send you to your vet's office. Often it happens in the fall, after the furnace has come on, or during high pollen season, and seems to happen for no reason at all. I think some Griffons simply do it because it creates such a stir from their people!

Elongated Soft Palate and Collapsed Trachea

I have only rarely seen a Brussels Griffon with an elongated soft palate, though it is common with brachycephalic breeds. The affected dog will have very little tolerance for heat and will pant noisily. If your veterinarian feels that the soft palate is fluttering about and restricting air flow into the trachea, it can be surgically shortened.

Collapsed trachea is a weakening and flattening of the tube that carries air to the lungs and it can be either inherited or caused by damage to the trachea from persistent, chronic coughing or injury. Never use a choke chain collar for any reason on a dog suffering from a collapsed trachea; in fact such a dog would be more comfortable wearing a harness. The dog can also be made more comfortable with the use of bronchial dilators and cough suppressants as he ages and he should live in a smoke-free environment.

Heatstroke

Dogs do not have sweat glands as we do. They perspire from the pads of their feet and by panting. As a consequence, dogs, especially those with flat faces, can overheat very easily. Sadly, many dogs die of heatstroke every year and many of those tragedies are completely avoidable. Take a lesson from those grim statistics and never leave your dog in a parked car. If your Griff displays rapid, shallow breathing and a rapid heartbeat, find ice or cold water immediately (even from a garden hose), wet him thoroughly and rush him to an emergency clinic.

While air conditioning in hot climates is certainly nice for your Griffon, it makes him even more sensitive to heat when he is outdoors. Dark dogs are more susceptible to heatstroke than lighter-colored ones, but heatstroke can affect dogs of all colors in a surprising variety of weather conditions.

Pneumonia

Pneumonia can happen quickly with brachycephalic Toy breeds, and must immediately be taken seriously. If your Griffon has become chilled and seems not to feel well, or if he has aspirated some form of liquid, monitor his breathing and temperature carefully, and take him to your vet at the first indication of trouble.

Bee Stings

Some dogs are highly allergic to bee stings, as are some people. Unfortunately, you won't know if your dog is sensitive until he has a reaction. If you have left your dog alone in the yard while "running to the store," you may not know until it is too late. If your Griffon's face starts to swell, or he becomes depressed and very quiet, check his gums (they should be pink) and examine his whole body for welts. Griffons often are stung in the mouth or front feet because of their cat-like, playful nature. If the mouth is swelling but the dog can still swallow, liquify Benadryl® or other antihistamine and rush him to your vet. If the sting is less severe, remove the stinger, if you can find it, and put a drop of pure bleach on the wound; this will neutralize the pain.

Lameness

Once Brussels Griffons are past the usual perils of the newborn and the very young, they do very well. Most, in fact, achieve a ripe, old age. They are able to go to their new homes, and are generally quite hardy and healthy as a breed. They are susceptible to the usual Toy dog maladies, such as luxating patellas (kneecaps sliding out of line) or Legg-Perthes' disease (necrotic degeneration of the femoral head), which becomes evident at about 6 or 7 months of age, but there are no conditions specific to the Brussels Griffon that other Toy breeds don't occasionally also have. While hip dysplasia is not usually a debilitating disease in small breeds because of their light weight, I have heard of a few cases in Brussels Griffons. If your Griffon persists in walking with a "bunny hop," have his hips x-rayed— to be sure of any causitive agent.

Any persistent limping should be checked by your veterinarian, unless you can determine that it is caused by a shallow cut, bee sting or a foreign body lodged in the foot that you can tend to yourself. Broken nails may bleed profusely and may need to be cauterized by your vet. It is always important to keep your Griffon in trim condition. If he has a tendency to bone, joint or muscle problems, it is imperative for his continuing health that he is not allowed to become overweight. If he has a mild case of luxating patellas or hip dysplasia and is not overweight, he will probably live out his life in reasonable comfort. If these problems are severe and are causing him pain, or if he has Legg-Perthes' disease, he will need surgery to lead a normally active life.

Hypoglycemia (Low Blood Sugar)

It is not uncommon for Toy dogs to wobble when they walk and then to "go limp" from low blood sugar after a strenuous play session. Hypoglycemia may also lead to seizures, so if your puppy is prone to this problem, keep a squirt bottle of Karo™ syrup handy and squirt a little in his mouth at the first sign of weakness (or during a seizure). If these episodes are a problem for your Griffon, be sure that he eats a little food, *often*. Most dogs will outgrow this condition as their body fat increases.

Urinary Tract Infections

If your dog tries to urinate more frequently than normal and very little urine, or bloody urine, is produced, he may have a urinary tract infection. Well-housetrained animals affected with a urinary tract infection will often urinate in the house unexpectedly. When you take him to your veterinarian, please ask for a culture on the urine. This is one infection that easily becomes chronic if it is not treated long enough or with the correct antibiotic.

Poisonous Plants and Toxic Substances

Your Griffon, that perpetual 2-year-old child, will taste almost everything. It is a natural sense for a dog. The problem with this comes from the many poisonous plants and substances around most houses and yards. Become familiar with the plants in your area and read all the labels on your cleaners, cosmetics and other household products. Consider, it takes very little antifreeze to kill a dog, and it is evidently sweet-tasting and can be licked up from a parking space or garage floor.

Signs of poisoning include vomiting, salivation and convulsions. Call your vet at once, as well as the National Animal Poison Control Center at 1-900-680-0000 whenever you are faced with an instance of poisoning.

Emergencies and First Aid

Animal bites should be soaked with hydrogen peroxide, pressure applied to control bleeding and the dog rushed to the vet. If a wild animal bit your Griffon, inform your local animal control officer with any information that you have. The animal may have been rabid.

Bleeding, shock or fracture victims must be rushed to an emergency vet clinic. Apply direct pressure over the site of any bleeding. A dog in shock may pant or be semiconscious and have glazed eyes with pale gums. If there is a chance of broken bones, slide the dog very carefully on to a flat surface and rush him to the nearest clinic.

Choking requires immediate action on your part. With your finger, you must quickly find and dislodge the object causing the problem. If you can't find it, rush your Griffon to the vet. Prevention is the bottom line here. Always watch for toys, small rawhide chews and other items your Griffon could choke on. Have your vet instruct you on the Heimlich maneuver for dogs so you will know how to use it if the need arises.

Allergies in Griffons most often show up on the skin. Some dogs are allergic to grasses, some to fleas and some have food allergies. Certain new carpets are so chemically treated that they cause allergic problems in people as well as pets. Shop for carpets carefully because your dog lives closer to your floor than you do. Most veterinarians can guess pretty accurately about allergies, but tests are also available that can be done

A FIRST-AID KIT

Keep a canine first-aid kit on hand for general care and emergencies. Check it periodically to make sure liquids haven't spilled or dried up, and replace medications and materials after they're used. Your kit should include:

Activated charcoal tablets

Adhesive tape
(1 and 2 inches wide)

Antibacterial ointment
(for skin and eyes)

Aspirin (buffered or enteric coated, *not* Ibuprofen)

Bandages: Gauze rolls (1 and 2 inches wide) and dressing pads

Cotton balls

Diarrhea medicine

Dosing syringe

Hydrogen peroxide (3%)

Petroleum jelly

Rectal thermometer

Rubber gloves

Rubbing alcohol

Scissors

Tourniquet

Towel

Tweezers

and the appropriate antigen can be administered. Beware of giving your Griffon cortisone on a regular basis. This stops irritations miraculously, but it only masks the problem, and it can cause health damage to your dog.

Diarrhea is usually the normal result when your Griffon eats something he shouldn't. It is not always best to try to "stop him up" unless he is in danger of dehydrating. Feed rice for twenty-four hours to clear the condition. If it persists past twenty-four hours, or turns bloody or to mucous, it can be a symptom of some very serious problems, so seek veterinary attention before your Griff dehydrates.

Vomiting, like diarrhea, is usually from the wrong choice of tidbit, and it is treated with a mild diet for twenty-four hours. If it persists, turns bloody or your Griffon looks lethargic, get him to the vet in a hurry.

Liquid Medication

Water down maple syrup, ice cream or something your dog would find very tasty, and occasionally let him try it with the following method so he will be used to it when you must give medicine. This is given with an eye dropper or syringe with the needle removed. Do not try to use a teaspoon. Carefully measure the amount prescribed. Sit on a straight chair and hold the Griffon on your lap, facing out with his back against your abdomen. With your left wrist, gently press his neck against your body, which should also cause him to point his face up toward yours. You can cuddle or scratch him and talk to him while you do this. All the while, tell him, "This is yummy!" With your left hand, pull the right corner of his mouth out a little and insert the dropper as far to the back molars as you can with your right hand. By doing this, his lips should form a little pouch.

Slowly dispense the liquid into the corner of his mouth while speaking to him in a soothing voice. If the medication runs out, you are either going too fast, his face isn't tipped up or he is not swallowing. If he isn't swallowing, hold his face up with one hand and stroke his throat with a light downward touch until you feel him swallow. If his natural Griffon stubbornness *never* gives him the feeling that he is being forced to do this, and you practice with a treat he really likes, this should be an easy procedure to use for future needs.

Giving Pills

Griffons are *very smart*. If you need to give pills, it is best that you *never* let him know that he took the first (or any subsequent) pill. Giving pills must be taken very seriously and only attempted by a person sure to succeed in fooling the Griff by variations of the following

To give a pill, open the mouth wide, then drop it in the back of the throat.

method: If you have another animal, lure him nearby and feed him *tiny* bits of the "patient's" favorite food. This should be something that he only rarely gets and it should have a irresistible odor! Liverwurst is a favorite, some like peanut butter (my dogs yawn), some like tiny bits of cheese (Brie is high on their favorites list) or salami—whatever turns your "Griffon."

Giving Eye Medication

To medicate a Griffon's eyes, take hold of the bottom eyelid with your left hand and gently pull the lid down to prevent the eye from closing. With a Rough, hold the outer hair just below the eye. With your right hand holding the medicine, put the heel of your hand on

Squeeze eye ointment into the lower lid.

top of the dog's head and pull toward the neck to hold the skin tight to further prevent the eye from closing. In this position, gently insert the medicine. If you are right-handed and treating the left eye, have someone else hold the Griffon so that he is facing you and use the heel of your left hand on top of his head while your right hand

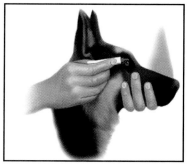

drops in the medicine and the little finger pulls down the bottom lid. You can get to be quite good

An Elizabethan collar keeps your dog from licking a fresh wound.

at this; hopefully, you will never have enough need to become an expert!

Ears—To Crop or Not to Crop

I personally would not advise cropping the ears of a pet Griffon. For a show dog, I would wait at until he was at least 1 year of age if there was any question about his head growing into his ears. Some people prefer the look of Griffons with their ears cropped; others prefer

the natural look. I think natural ears are adorable and add to a Griffon's expression, but this is a personal choice. If you choose to crop, once again, choose a veterinarian who has had great success with anesthesia in brachycephalic breeds, and perhaps the ears can be done at the same time you spay or neuter, or remove baby canine teeth.

Spaying and Neutering

If you have a bitch, please don't feel that your Griffon will be missing something if she does not get to have puppies. She does not need a canine family to be complete; she has her human family and that is enough for her. Griffon survival is often fragile until puppies are weaned. So often "breeding a litter for the kids" leads to disaster for everyone, especially the children. I would advise spaying or neutering at the earliest age that your vet feels comfortable doing the surgery. This can now be done when a puppy is quite young as health authorities are finding extra benefits for dogs that are spayed or neutered early.

As for the pet male Griffon, he will be so much better off neutered. That Griffon boy you took into your home as your special friend will never miss what he never experiences. Also, how much attention do you suppose an unaltered male will give you if he knows there is a female in heat nearby? A neutered male will never experience the frustration of being near females he is not allowed to breed, and will never feel the need to compete with other males. He will not be subject to some of the disorders that come to entire dogs in later life, and his inactive hormones will not scream at him to scent mark in his home. Speak to your veterinarian and find out the best time to have your Griffon neutered and be guided by his or her recommendations. You and your Griffon will both come out ahead, believe me.

Care of the Aging Brussels Griffon

There is nothing more dear than an older beloved friend. He has given a lifetime of love and devotion and now he needs special attention and care. He probably won't see or hear as well, may have more dental problems and he certainly won't be as fast on his feet. Because he will be spending more time resting, it is important that his bed be very soft, comfortable, warm and in an area where he can be close to you and other household activity. Now you can buy heated water beds for pets, but we made one years ago and it was the ideal situation for our arthritic 16-year-old. She basically lived the last three years of her life lounging in her heated water bed.

It is very important not to let an older Griffon become overweight, but feed at least twice a day a senior formula kibble or a special diet your vet has prescribed. Keep track of his eating so you will be alert if he slacks off his food because of a possible health problem. Don't think he must have canned food because he no longer has teeth. You'll be surprised how easily he will gum down his kibble. He must always have fresh water available where it will be easy for him to find and he must drink adequate amounts of water.

ADVANTAGES OF SPAY/NEUTER

The greatest advantage of spaying (for females) or neutering (for males) your dog is that you are guaranteed your dog will not produce puppies. There are too many puppies already available for too few homes. There are other advantages as well.

ADVANTAGES OF SPAYING

No messy heats.

No "suitors" howling at your windows or waiting in your yard.

Decreased incidences of pyometra (disease of the uterus) and breast cancer.

ADVANTAGES OF NEUTERING

Lessens male aggressive and territorial behaviors, but doesn't affect the dog's personality. Behaviors are often owner-induced, so neutering is not the only answer, but it is a good start.

Prevents the need to roam in search of bitches in season.

Decreased incidences of urogenital diseases.

You *must* also keep special watch on the feet of the geriatric. The joint stiffness will be enough for him to deal with; he will not need the added pain and toe distortion of long toenails or foreign objects lodged between his pads.

Most Toy dogs live to a ripe, old age, and meeting your aging Griffon's health needs will help you both to enjoy his senior years.

Do not neglect his appearance or hygiene during this special time in his life. It is more important than ever that he enjoy smelling sweet and being handled and loved! Your daily contact with his skin, eyes, ears and teeth will help alert you to changes that your vet may be able to help with.

Euthanasia

There is a time to do all within your power to continue your beloved companion's life and there is a time to let him go. It is so unfair to ask your Griffon, who has nothing but devotion for you, to continue his life when the quality has gone and been replaced with pain, just because you wish to keep him alive for you. Even with the many new drugs now that make arthritis and other maladies of aging more bearable, this time will come. This is a very difficult and personal choice, but when you do make the decision to give your Griffon peace, please give him the comfort of your love and presence. It may be most traumatic for you, but he deserves to peacefully go to sleep in your familiar arms, hearing your voice. You will find comfort witnessing the ease with which his sleep comes and knowing that you did what was best for him as your final testament of love.

Your Happy, Healthy Pet

Your Dog's Name _____

Name on Your Dog's Pedigree (if your dog has one) _____

_____

Where Your Dog Came From _____

_____

Your Dog's Birthday _____

Your Dog's Veterinarian

    Name _____

    Address _____

    Phone Number_____

    Emergency Number_____

Your Dog's Health

    Vaccines

    type _____ date given _____

    type _____ date given _____

    type _____ date given _____

    type _____ date given _____

    Heartworm

    date tested _____ type used_____ start date _____

Your Dog's License Number_____

Groomer's Name and Number _____

Dogsitter/Walker's Name and Number_____

Awards Your Dog Has Won

    Award _____ date earned _____

    Award _____ date earned _____

part three

Enjoying
your
Dog

Basic
Training

by Ian Dunbar, Ph.D., MRCVS

Training is the jewel in the crown—the most important aspect of doggy husbandry. There is no more important variable influencing dog behavior and temperament than the dog's education: A well-trained, well-behaved and good-natured puppydog is always a joy to live with, but an untrained and uncivilized dog can be a perpetual nightmare. Moreover, deny the dog an education and she will not have the opportunity to fulfill her own canine potential; neither will she have the ability to communicate effectively with her human companions.

Luckily, modern psychological training methods are easy, efficient, effective and, above all, considerably dog-friendly and user-friendly.

Doggy education is as simple as it is enjoyable. But before you can have a good time play-training with your new dog, you have to learn what to do and how to do it. There is no bigger variable influencing the success of dog training than the *owner's* experience and expertise. *Before you embark on the dog's education, you must first educate yourself.*

Basic Training for Owners

Ideally, basic owner training should begin well *before* you select your dog. Find out all you can about your chosen breed first, then master rudimentary training and handling skills. If you already have your puppy-dog, owner training is a dire emergency—the clock is ticking! Especially for puppies, the first few weeks at home are the most important and influential days in the dog's life. Indeed, the cause of most adolescent and adult problems may be traced back to the initial days the pup explores her new home. This is the time to establish the *status quo*—to teach the puppydog how you would like her to behave and so prevent otherwise quite predictable problems.

In addition to consulting breeders and breed books such as this one (which understandably have a positive breed bias), seek out as many pet owners with your breed as you can find. Good points are obvious. What you want to find out are the breed-specific *problems,* so you can nip them in the bud. In particular, you should talk to owners with *adolescent* dogs and make a list of all anticipated problems. Most important, *test drive* at least half a dozen adolescent and adult dogs of your breed yourself. An 8-week-old puppy is deceptively easy to handle, but she will acquire adult size, speed and strength in just four months, so you should learn now what to prepare for.

Puppy and pet dog training classes offer a convenient venue to locate pet owners and observe dogs in action. For a list of suitable trainers in your area, contact the Association of Pet Dog Trainers (see chapter 13). You may also begin your basic owner training by observing other owners in class. Watch as many classes and test drive as many dogs as possible. Select an upbeat, dog-friendly, people-friendly, fun-and-games, puppydog pet training class to learn the ropes. Also, watch training videos and read training books. You must find out what to do and how to do it *before* you have to do it.

Principles of Training

Most people think training comprises teaching the dog to do things such as sit, speak and roll over, but even a 4-week-old pup knows how to do these things already. Instead, the first step in training involves teaching the dog human words for each dog behavior and activity and for each aspect of the dog's environment. That way you, the owner, can more easily participate in the dog's domestic education by directing her to perform specific actions appropriately, that is, at the right time, in the right place and so on. Training opens communication channels, enabling an educated dog to at least understand her owner's requests.

In addition to teaching a dog *what* we want her to do, it is also necessary to teach her *why* she should do what we ask. Indeed, 95 percent of training revolves around motivating the dog *to want to do* what we want. Dogs often understand what their owners want; they just don't see the point of doing it—especially when the owner's repetitively boring and seemingly senseless instructions are totally at odds with much more pressing and exciting doggy distractions. It is not so much the dog that is being stubborn or dominant; rather, it is the owner who has failed to acknowledge the dog's needs and feelings and to approach training from the dog's point of view.

THE MEANING OF INSTRUCTIONS

The secret to successful training is learning how to use training lures to predict or prompt specific behaviors—to coax the dog to do what you want *when* you want. Any highly valued object (such as a treat or toy) may be used as a lure, which the dog will follow with her eyes and nose. Moving the lure in specific ways entices the dog to move her nose, head and entire body in specific ways. In fact, by learning the art of manipulating various lures, it is possible to teach the dog to assume virtually any body position and perform any action. Once you have control over the expression of the dog's behaviors and can elicit any body position or behavior at will, you can easily teach the dog to perform on request.

Teach your dog words for each activity she needs to know, like down.

Tell your dog what you want her to do, use a lure to entice her to respond correctly, then profusely praise and maybe reward her once she performs the desired action. For example, verbally request "Tina, sit!" while you move a squeaky toy upwards and backwards over the dog's muzzle (lure-movement and hand signal), smile knowingly as she looks up (to follow the lure) and sits down (as a result of canine anatomical engineering), then praise her to distraction ("Gooood Tina!"). Squeak the toy, offer a training treat and give your dog and yourself a pat on the back.

Being able to elicit desired responses over and over enables the owner to reward the dog over and over. Consequently, the dog begins to think training is fun. For example, the more the dog is rewarded for sitting, the more she enjoys sitting. Eventually the dog comes to realize that, whereas most sitting is appreciated, sitting immediately upon request usually prompts especially enthusiastic praise and a slew of high-level rewards. The dog begins to sit on cue much of the time, showing that she is starting to grasp the meaning of the owner's verbal request and hand signal.

WHY COMPLY?

Most dogs enjoy initial lure-reward training and are only too happy to comply with their owners' wishes. Unfortunately, repetitive drilling without appreciative feedback tends to diminish the dog's enthusiasm until she eventually fails to see the point of complying anymore. Moreover, as the dog approaches adolescence she becomes more easily distracted as she develops other interests. Lengthy sessions with repetitive exercises tend to bore and demotivate both parties. If it's not fun, the owner doesn't do it and neither does the dog.

Integrate training into your dog's life: The greater number of training sessions each day and the *shorter* they are, the more willingly compliant your dog will become. Make sure to have a short (just a few seconds) training interlude before every enjoyable canine activity. For example, ask your dog to sit to greet people, to sit before you throw her Frisbee and to sit for her supper. Really, sitting is no different from a canine "Please."

To train your dog, you need gentle hands, a loving heart and a good attitude.

Also, include numerous short training interludes during every enjoyable canine pastime, for example, when playing with the dog or when she is running in the park. In this fashion, doggy distractions may be effectively converted into rewards for training. Just as all games have rules, fun becomes training . . . and training becomes fun.

Eventually, rewards actually become unnecessary to continue motivating your dog. If trained with consideration and kindness, performing the desired behaviors will become self-rewarding and, in a sense, your dog will motivate herself. Just as it is not necessary to reward a human companion during an enjoyable walk in the park, or following a game of tennis, it is hardly necessary to reward our best friend—the dog— for walking by our side or while playing fetch. Human company during enjoyable activities is reward enough for most dogs.

Even though your dog has become self-motivating, it's still good to praise and pet her a lot and offer rewards once in a while, especially for a good job well done. And if for no other reason, praising and rewarding others is good for the human heart.

PUNISHMENT

Without a doubt, lure-reward training is by far the best way to teach: Entice your dog to do what you want and then reward her for doing so. Unfortunately, a human shortcoming is to take the good for granted and to moan and groan at the bad. Specifically, the dog's many good behaviors are ignored while the owner focuses on punishing the dog for making mistakes. In extreme cases, instruction is *limited* to punishing mistakes made by a trainee dog, child, employee or husband, even though it has been proven punishment training is notoriously inefficient and ineffective and is decidedly unfriendly and combative. It teaches the dog that training is a drag, almost as quickly as it teaches the dog to dislike her trainer. Why treat our best friends like our worst enemies?

Punishment training is also much more laborious and time consuming. Whereas it takes only a finite amount of time to teach a dog what to chew, for example, it takes much, much longer to punish the dog for each and every mistake. Remember, *there is only one right way!* So why not teach that right way from the outset?!

103

To make matters worse, punishment training causes severe lapses in the dog's reliability. Since it is obviously impossible to punish the dog each and every time she misbehaves, the dog quickly learns to distinguish between those times when she must comply (so as to avoid impending punishment) and those times when she need not comply, because punishment is impossible. Such times include when the dog is off leash and 6 feet away, when the owner is otherwise engaged (talking to a friend, watching television, taking a shower, tending to the baby or chatting on the telephone) or when the dog is left at home alone.

Instances of misbehavior will be numerous when the owner is away, because even when the dog complied in the owner's looming presence, she did so unwillingly. The dog was forced to act against her will, rather than molding her will to want to please. Hence, when the owner is absent, not only does the dog know she need not comply, she simply does not want to. Again, the trainee is not a stubborn vindictive beast, but rather the trainer has failed to teach. Punishment training invariably creates unpredictable Jekyll and Hyde behavior.

Trainer's Tools

Many training books extol the virtues of a vast array of training paraphernalia and electronic and metallic gizmos, most of which are designed for canine restraint, correction and punishment, rather than for actual facilitation of doggy education. In reality, most effective training tools are not found in stores; they come from within ourselves. In addition to a willing dog, all you really need is a functional human brain, gentle hands, a loving heart and a good attitude.

In terms of equipment, all dogs do require a quality buckle collar to sport dog tags and to attach the leash (for safety and to comply with local leash laws). Hollow chew toys (like Kongs or sterilized longbones) and a dog bed or collapsible crate are musts for housetraining. Three additional tools are required:

1. specific lures (training treats and toys) to predict and prompt specific desired behaviors;

2. rewards (praise, affection, training treats and toys) to reinforce for the dog what a lot of fun it all is; and

3. knowledge—how to convert the dog's favorite activities and games (potential distractions to training) into "life-rewards," which may be employed to facilitate training.

The most powerful of these is *knowledge*. Education is the key! Watch training classes, participate in training classes, watch videos, read books, enjoy play-training with your dog and then your dog will say "Please," and your dog will say "Thank you!"

Housetraining

If dogs were left to their own devices, certainly they would chew, dig and bark for entertainment and then no doubt highlight a few areas of their living space with sprinkles of urine, in much the same way we decorate by hanging pictures. Consequently, when we ask a dog to live with us, we must teach her *where* she may dig, *where* she may perform her toilet duties, *what* she may chew and *when* she may bark. After all, when left at home alone for many hours, we cannot expect the dog to amuse herself by completing crosswords or watching the soaps on TV!

Also, it would be decidedly unfair to keep the house rules a secret from the dog, and then get angry and punish the poor critter for inevitably transgressing rules she did not even know existed. Remember: Without adequate education and guidance, the dog will be forced to establish her own rules—doggy rules—and most probably will be at odds with the owner's view of domestic living.

Since most problems develop during the first few days the dog is at home, prospective dog owners must be certain they are quite clear about the principles of housetraining *before* they get a dog. Early misbehaviors quickly become established as the *status quo*—

becoming firmly entrenched as hard-to-break bad habits, which set the precedent for years to come. Make sure to teach your dog good habits right from the start. Good habits are just as hard to break as bad ones!

Ideally, when a new dog comes home, try to arrange for someone to be present as much as possible during the first few days (for adult dogs) or weeks for puppies. With only a little forethought, it is surprisingly easy to find a puppy sitter, such as a retired person, who would be willing to eat from your refrigerator and watch your television while keeping an eye on the newcomer to encourage the dog to play with chew toys and to ensure she goes outside on a regular basis.

POTTY TRAINING

To teach the dog where to relieve herself:

1. never let her make a single mistake;
2. let her know where you want her to go; and
3. handsomely reward her for doing so:
   "GOOOOOOOD DOG!!!" liver treat, liver treat, liver treat!

Preventing Mistakes

A single mistake is a training disaster, since it heralds many more in future weeks. And each time the dog soils the house, this further reinforces the dog's unfortunate preference for an indoor, carpeted toilet. *Do not let an unhousetrained dog have full run of the house.*

When you are away from home, or cannot pay full attention, confine the dog to an area where elimination is appropriate, such as an outdoor run or, better still, a small, comfortable indoor kennel with access to an outdoor run. When confined in this manner, most dogs will naturally housetrain themselves.

If that's not possible, confine the dog to an area, such as a utility room, kitchen, basement or garage, where elimination may not be desired in the long run but as an interim measure it is certainly preferable to doing it all around the house. Use newspaper to cover the floor of the dog's day room. The newspaper may be used to soak up the urine and to wrap up and dispose of the feces. Once your dog develops a preferred spot for eliminating, it is only necessary to cover that part of the floor with newspaper. The smaller papered area may then be moved (only a little each day) towards the door to the outside. Thus the dog will develop the tendency to go to the door when she needs to relieve herself.

Never confine an unhousetrained dog to a crate for long periods. Doing so would force the dog to soil the crate and ruin its usefulness as an aid for housetraining (see the following discussion).

Teaching Where

In order to teach your dog where you would like her to do her business, you have to be there to direct the proceedings—an obvious, yet often neglected, fact of life. In order to be there to teach the dog *where* to go, you need to know *when* she needs to go. Indeed, the success of housetraining depends on the owner's ability to predict these times. Certainly, a regular feeding schedule will facilitate prediction somewhat, but there is nothing like "loading the deck" and influencing the timing of the outcome yourself!

Whenever you are at home, make sure the dog is under constant supervision and/or confined to a small

The first few weeks at home are the most important and influential in your dog's life.

area. If already well trained, simply instruct the dog to lie down in her bed or basket. Alternatively, confine the dog to a crate (doggy den) or tie-down (a short, 18-inch lead that can be clipped to an eye hook in the baseboard near her bed). Short-term close confinement strongly inhibits urination and defecation, since the dog does not want to soil her sleeping area. Thus, when you release the puppydog each hour, she will definitely need to urinate immediately and defecate every third or fourth hour. Keep the dog confined to her doggy den and take her to her intended toilet area each hour, every hour and on the hour.

When taking your dog outside, instruct her to sit quietly before opening the door—she will soon learn to sit by the door when she needs to go out!

Teaching Why

Being able to predict when the dog needs to go enables the owner to be on the spot to praise and reward the dog. Each hour, hurry the dog to the intended toilet area in the yard, issue the appropriate instruction ("Go pee!" or "Go poop!"), then give the dog three to four minutes to produce. Praise and offer a couple of training treats when successful. The treats are important because many people fail to praise their dogs with feeling . . . and housetraining is hardly the time for understatement. So either loosen up and enthusiastically praise that dog: "Wuzzzer-wuzzer-wuzzer, hoooser good wuffer den? Hoooo went pee for Daddy?" Or say "Good dog!" as best you can and offer the treats for effect.

Following elimination is an ideal time for a spot of play-training in the yard or house. Also, an empty dog may be allowed greater freedom around the house for the next half hour or so, just as long as you keep an eye out to make sure she does not get into other kinds of mischief. If you are preoccupied and cannot pay full attention, confine the dog to her doggy den once more to enjoy a peaceful snooze or to play with her many chew toys.

If your dog does not eliminate within the allotted time outside—no biggie! Back to her doggy den, and then try again after another hour.

As I own large dogs, I always feel more relaxed walking an empty dog, knowing that I will not need to finish our stroll weighted down with bags of feces!

Beware of falling into the trap of walking the dog to get her to eliminate. The good ol' dog walk is such an enormous highlight in the dog's life that it represents the single biggest potential reward in domestic dogdom. However, when in a hurry, or during inclement weather, many owners abruptly terminate the walk the moment the dog has done her business. This, in effect, severely punishes the dog for doing the right thing, in the right place at the right time. Consequently, many dogs become strongly inhibited from eliminating outdoors because they know it will signal an abrupt end to an otherwise thoroughly enjoyable walk.

Instead, instruct the dog to relieve herself in the yard prior to going for a walk. If you follow the above instructions, most dogs soon learn to eliminate on cue. As soon as the dog eliminates, praise (and offer a treat or two)—"Good dog! Let's go walkies!" Use the walk as a reward for eliminating in the yard. If the dog does not go, put her back in her doggy den and think about a walk later on. You will find with a "No feces—no walk" policy, your dog will become one of the fastest defecators in the business.

If you do not have a backyard, instruct the dog to eliminate right outside your front door prior to the walk. Not only will this facilitate clean up and disposal of the feces in your own trash can but, also, the walk may again be used as a colossal reward.

CHEWING AND BARKING

Short-term close confinement also teaches the dog that occasional quiet moments are a reality of domestic living. Your puppydog is extremely impressionable during her first few weeks at home. Regular confinement at this time soon exerts a calming influence over the dog's personality. Remember, once the dog is housetrained and calmer, there will be a whole lifetime ahead for the dog to enjoy full run of the house and garden. On the other hand, by letting the newcomer have unrestricted access to the entire household and allowing her to run willy-nilly, she will most certainly develop a bunch of behavior problems in short order, no doubt necessitating confinement later in life. It would not be fair to remedially restrain and confine a dog you have trained, through neglect, to run free.

When confining the dog, make sure she always has an impressive array of suitable chew toys. Kongs and sterilized longbones (both readily available from pet stores) make the best chew toys, since they are hollow and may be stuffed with treats to heighten the dog's interest. For example, by stuffing the little hole at the top of a Kong with a small piece of freeze-dried liver, the dog will not want to leave it alone.

Remember, treats do not have to be junk food and they certainly should not represent extra calories. Rather, treats should be part of each dog's regular daily diet: Some food may be served in the dog's bowl for breakfast and dinner, some food may be used as training treats, and some food may be used for stuffing chew toys. I regularly stuff my dogs' many Kongs with different shaped biscuits and kibble.

Make sure your puppy has suitable chew toys.

The kibble seems to fall out fairly easily, as do the oval-shaped biscuits, thus rewarding the dog instantaneously for checking out the chew toys. The bone-shaped biscuits fall out after a while, rewarding the dog for worrying at the chew toy. But the triangular biscuits never come out. They remain inside the Kong as lures, maintaining the dog's fascination with her chew toy. To further focus the dog's interest, I always make sure to flavor the triangular biscuits by rubbing them with a little cheese or freeze-dried liver.

If stuffed chew toys are reserved especially for times the dog is confined, the puppydog will soon learn to enjoy quiet moments in her doggy den and she will quickly develop a chew-toy habit— a good habit! This is a simple *autoshaping* process; all the owner has to do is set up the situation and the dog all but trains herself— easy and effective. Even when the dog is given run of the house, her first inclination will be to indulge her rewarding chew-toy habit rather than destroy less-attractive household articles, such as curtains, carpets, chairs and compact disks. Similarly, a chew-toy chewer will be less inclined to scratch and chew herself excessively. Also, if the dog busies herself as a recreational chewer, she will be less inclined to develop into a recreational barker or digger when left at home alone.

Stuff a number of chew toys whenever the dog is left confined and remove the extra-special-tasting treats when you return. Your dog will now amuse herself with her chew toys before falling asleep and then resume playing with her chew toys when she expects you to return. Since most owner-absent misbehavior happens right after you leave and right before your expected return, your puppydog will now be conveniently preoccupied with her chew toys at these times.

Come and Sit

Most puppies will happily approach virtually anyone, whether called or not; that is, until they collide with adolescence and

To teach come, call your dog, open your arms as a welcoming signal, wave a toy or a treat and praise for every step in your direction.

develop other more important doggy interests, such as sniffing a multiplicity of exquisite odors on the grass. Your mission, Mr./Ms. Owner, is to teach and reward the pup for coming reliably, willingly and happily when called—and you have just three months to get it done. Unless adequately reinforced, your puppy's tendency to approach people will self-destruct by adolescence.

Call your dog ("Tina, come!"), open your arms (and maybe squat down) as a welcoming signal, waggle a treat or toy as a lure and reward the puppydog when she comes running. Do not wait to praise the dog until she reaches you—she may come 95 percent of the way and then run off after some distraction. Instead, praise the dog's *first* step towards you and continue praising enthusiastically for *every* step she takes in your direction.

When the rapidly approaching puppy dog is three lengths away from impact, instruct her to sit ("Tina, sit!") and hold the lure in front of you in an outstretched hand to prevent her from hitting you midchest and knocking you flat on your back! As Tina decelerates to nose the lure, move the treat upwards and backwards just over her muzzle with an upwards motion of your extended arm (palm-upwards). As the dog looks up to follow the lure, she will sit down (if she jumps up, you are holding the lure too high). Praise the dog for sitting. Move backwards and call her again. Repeat this many times over, always praising when Tina comes and sits; on occasion, reward her.

For the first couple of trials, use a training treat both as a lure to entice the dog to come and sit and as a reward for doing so. Thereafter, try to use different items as lures and rewards. For example, lure the dog with a Kong or Frisbee but reward her with a food treat. Or lure the dog with a food treat but pat her and throw a tennis ball as a reward. After just a few repetitions, dispense with the lures and rewards; the dog will begin to respond willingly to your verbal requests and hand signals just for the prospect of praise from your heart and affection from your hands.

Instruct every family member, friend and visitor how to get the dog to come and sit. Invite people over for a series of pooch parties; do not keep the pup a secret— let other people enjoy this puppy, and let the pup enjoy other people. Puppydog parties are not only fun, they easily attract a lot of people to help *you* train *your* dog. Unless you teach your dog how to meet people, that is, to sit for greetings, no doubt the dog will resort to jumping up. Then you and the visitors will get annoyed, and the dog will be punished. This is not fair. *Send out those invitations for puppy parties and teach your dog to be mannerly and socially acceptable.*

Even though your dog quickly masters obedient recalls in the house, her reliability may falter when playing in the backyard or local park. Ironically, it is *the owner* who has unintentionally trained the dog *not* to respond in these instances. By allowing the dog to play and run around and otherwise have a good time, but then to call the dog to put her on leash to take her home, the dog quickly learns playing is fun but training is a drag. Thus, playing in the park becomes a severe distraction, which works against training. Bad news!

Instead, whether playing with the dog off leash or on leash, request her to come at frequent intervals—say, every minute or so. On most occasions, praise and pet the dog for a few seconds while she is sitting, then tell her to go play again. For especially fast recalls, offer a couple of training treats and take the time to praise and pet the dog enthusiastically before releasing her. The dog will learn that coming when called is not necessarily the end of the play session, and neither is it the end of the world; rather, it signals an enjoyable, quality time-out with the owner before resuming play once more. In fact, playing in the park now becomes a very effective life-reward, which works to facilitate training by reinforcing each obedient and timely recall. Good news!

Sit, Down, Stand and Rollover

Teaching the dog a variety of body positions is easy for owner and dog, impressive for spectators and extremely useful for all. Using lure-reward techniques, it is possible to train several positions at once to verbal commands or hand signals (which impress the socks off onlookers).

Sit and *down*—the two control commands—prevent or resolve nearly a hundred behavior problems. For example, if the dog happily and obediently sits or lies down when requested, she cannot jump on visitors, dash out the front door, run around and chase her tail, pester other dogs, harass cats or annoy family, friends or strangers. Additionally, "Sit" or "Down" are the best emergency commands for off-leash control.

It is easier to teach and maintain a reliable sit than maintain a reliable recall. *Sit* is the purest and simplest of commands—either the dog is sitting or she is not. If there is any change of circumstances or potential danger in the park, for example, simply instruct the dog to sit. If she sits, you have a number of options: Allow the dog to resume playing when she is safe, walk up and put the dog on leash or call the dog. The dog will be much more likely to come when called if she has already acknowledged her compliance by sitting. If the dog does not sit in the park—train her to!

Stand and *rollover-stay* are the two positions for examining the dog. Your veterinarian will love you to distraction if you take a little time to teach the dog to stand still and roll over and play possum. Also, your vet bills will be smaller because it will take the veterinarian less time to examine your dog. The rollover-stay is an especially useful command and is really just a variation of the down-stay: Whereas the dog lies prone in the traditional down, she lies supine in the rollover-stay.

As with teaching come and sit, the training techniques to teach the dog to assume all other body positions on cue are user-friendly and dog-friendly. Simply give the appropriate request, lure the dog into the desired body position using a training treat or toy and then *praise* (and maybe reward) the dog as soon as she complies. Try not to touch the dog to get her to respond. If you teach the dog by guiding her into position, the dog will quickly learn that rump-pressure means sit, for example, but as yet you still have no control over your dog if she is just 6 feet away. It will still be necessary to teach the dog to sit on request. So do not make training a time-consuming two-step process; instead, teach the dog to sit to a verbal request or hand signal from the outset. Once the dog sits willingly when requested, by all means use your hands to pet the dog when she does so.

To teach *down* when the dog is already sitting, say "Tina, down!," hold the lure in one hand (palm down) and lower that hand to the floor between the dog's forepaws. As the dog lowers her head to follow the lure, slowly move the lure away from the dog just a fraction (in front of her paws). The dog will lie down as she stretches her nose forward to follow the lure. Praise the dog when she does so. If the dog stands up, you pulled the lure away too far and too quickly.

When teaching the dog to lie down from the standing position, say "Down" and lower the lure to the floor as before. Once the dog has lowered her forequarters and assumed a play bow, gently and slowly move the lure *towards* the dog between her forelegs. Praise the dog as soon as her rear end plops down.

After just a couple of trials it will be possible to alternate sits and downs and have the dog energetically perform doggy push-ups. Praise the dog a lot, and after half a dozen or so push-ups reward the dog with a training treat or toy. You will notice the more energetically you move your arm—upwards (palm up) to get the dog to sit, and downwards (palm down) to get the dog to lie down—the more energetically the dog responds to your requests. Now try training the dog in silence and you will notice she has also learned to respond to hand signals. Yeah! Not too shabby for the first session.

To teach *stand* from the sitting position, say "Tina, stand," slowly move the lure half a dog-length away from the dog's nose, keeping it at nose level, and praise the dog as she stands to follow the lure. As soon

Using a food lure to teach sit, down and stand. 1) "Phoenix, sit." 2) Hand palm upwards, move lure up and back over dog's muzzle. 3) "Good sit, Phoenix!" 4) "Phoenix, down." 5) Hand palm downwards, move lure down to lie between dog's forepaws. 6) "Phoenix, off. Good down, Phoenix!" 7) "Phoenix, sit!" 8) Palm upwards, move lure up and back, keeping it close to dog's muzzle. 9) "Good sit, Phoenix!"

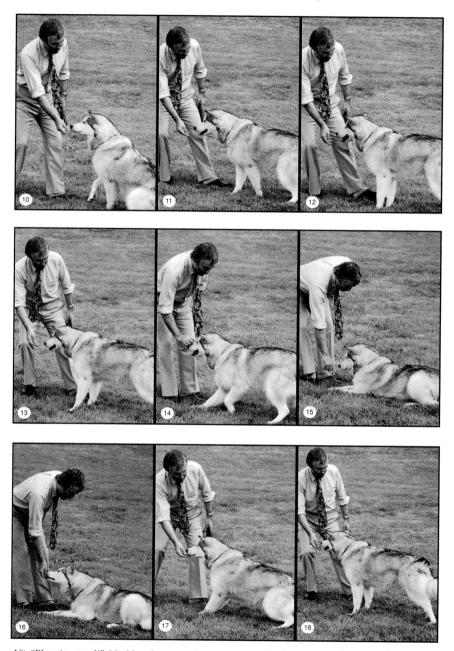

10) *"Phoenix, stand!"* 11) *Move lure away from dog at nose height, then lower it a tad.* 12) *"Phoenix, off! Good stand, Phoenix!"* 13) *"Phoenix, down!"* 14) *Hand palm downwards, move lure down to lie between dog's forepaws.* 15) *"Phoenix, off! Good down-stay, Phoenix!"* 16) *"Phoenix, stand!"* 17) *Move lure away from dog's muzzle up to nose height.* 18) *"Phoenix, off! Good stand-stay, Phoenix. Now we'll make the vet and groomer happy!"*

as the dog stands, lower the lure to just beneath the dog's chin to entice her to look down; otherwise she will stand and then sit immediately. To prompt the dog to stand from the down position, move the lure half a dog-length upwards and away from the dog, holding the lure at standing nose height from the floor.

Teaching *rollover* is best started from the down position, with the dog lying on one side, or at least with both hind legs stretched out on the same side. Say "Tina, bang!" and move the lure backwards and along-side the dog's muzzle to her elbow (on the side of her outstretched hind legs). Once the dog looks to the side and backwards, very slowly move the lure upwards to the dog's shoulder and backbone. Tickling the dog in the goolies (groin area) often invokes a reflex-raising of the hind leg as an appeasement gesture, which facil-itates the tendency to roll over. If you move the lure too quickly and the dog jumps into the standing posi-tion, have patience and start again. As soon as the dog rolls onto her back, keep the lure stationary and mes-merize the dog with a relaxing tummy rub.

To teach *rollover-stay* when the dog is standing or mov-ing, say "Tina, bang!" and give the appropriate hand signal (with index finger pointed and thumb cocked in true Sam Spade fashion), then in one fluid movement lure her to first lie down and then rollover-stay as above.

Teaching the dog to *stay* in each of the above four posi-tions becomes a piece of cake after first teaching the dog not to worry at the toy or treat training lure. This is best accomplished by hand feeding dinner kibble. Hold a piece of kibble firmly in your hand and softly instruct "Off!" Ignore any licking and slobbering *for however long the dog worries at the treat,* but say "Take it!" and offer the kibble *the instant* the dog breaks contact with her muzzle. Repeat this a few times, and then up the ante and insist the dog remove her muzzle for one whole second before offering the kibble. Then pro-gressively refine your criteria and have the dog not touch your hand (or treat) for longer and longer periods on each trial, such as for two seconds, four seconds, then six, ten, fifteen, twenty, thirty seconds and so on.

The dog soon learns: (1) worrying at the treat never gets results, whereas (2) noncontact is often rewarded after a variable time lapse.

Teaching *"Off!"* has many useful applications in its own right. Additionally, instructing the dog not to touch a training lure often produces spontaneous and magical stays. Request the dog to stand-stay, for example, and not to touch the lure. At first set your sights on a short two-second stay before rewarding the dog. (Remember, every long journey begins with a single step.) However, on subsequent trials, gradually and progressively increase the length of stay required to receive a reward. In no time at all your dog will stand calmly for a minute or so.

Relevancy Training

Once you have taught the dog what you expect her to do when requested to come, sit, lie down, stand, roll-over and stay, the time is right to teach the dog *why* she should comply with your wishes. The secret is to have many (*many*) extremely short training interludes (two to five seconds each) at numerous (*numerous*) times during the course of the dog's day. Especially work with the dog immediately *before* the dog's good times and *during* the dog's good times. For example, ask your dog to sit and/or lie down each time before opening doors, serving meals, offering treats and tummy rubs; ask the dog to perform a few controlled doggy push-ups before letting her off leash or throwing a tennis ball; and perhaps request the dog to sit-down-sit-stand-down-stand-rollover before inviting her to cuddle on the couch.

Similarly, request the dog to sit many times during play or on walks, and in no time at all the dog will be only too pleased to follow your instructions because she has learned that a compliant response heralds all sorts of goodies. Basically all you are trying to teach the dog is how to say please: "Please throw the tennis ball. Please may I snuggle on the couch."

Remember, it is important to keep training interludes short and to have many short sessions each and every day. The shortest (and most useful) session comprises asking the dog to sit and then go play during a play session. When trained this way, your dog will soon associate training with good times. In fact, the dog may be unable to distinguish between training and good times and, indeed, there should be no distinction. The warped concept that training involves forcing the dog to comply and/or dominating her will is totally at odds with the picture of a truly well-trained dog. In reality, enjoying a game of training with a dog is no different from enjoying a game of backgammon or tennis with a friend; and walking with a dog should be no different from strolling with a spouse, or with buddies on the golf course.

Walk by Your Side

Many people attempt to teach a dog to heel by putting her on a leash and physically correcting the dog when she makes mistakes. There are a number of things seriously wrong with this approach, the first being that most people do not want precision heeling; rather, they simply want the dog to follow or walk by their side. Second, when physically restrained during "training," even though the dog may grudgingly mope by your side when "handcuffed" on leash, let's see what happens when she is off leash. History! The dog is in the next county because she never enjoyed walking with you on leash and you have no control over her off leash. So let's just teach the dog off leash from the outset to *want* to walk with us. Third, if the dog has not been trained to heel, it is a trifle hasty to think about punishing the poor dog for making mistakes and breaking heeling rules she didn't even know existed. This is simply not fair! Surely, if the dog had been adequately taught how to heel, she would seldom make mistakes and hence there would be no need to correct the dog. Remember, each mistake and each correction (punishment) advertise the trainer's inadequacy, not the dog's. The dog is not stubborn, she is not stupid and she is not bad. Even if she were, she would still require training, so let's train her properly.

Let's teach the dog to *enjoy* following us and to *want* to walk by our side off leash. Then it will be easier to teach high-precision off-leash heeling patterns if desired. Before going on outdoor walks, it is necessary to teach the dog not to pull. Then it becomes easy to teach on-leash walking and heeling because the dog already wants to walk with you, she is familiar with the desired walking and heeling positions and she knows not to pull.

FOLLOWING

Start by training your dog to follow you. Many puppies will follow if you simply walk away from them and maybe click your fingers or chuckle. Adult dogs may require additional enticement to stimulate them to follow, such as a training lure or, at the very least, a lively trainer. To teach the dog to follow: (1) keep walking and (2) walk away from the dog. If the dog attempts to lead or lag, change pace; slow down if the dog forges too far ahead, but speed up if she lags too far behind. Say "Steady!" or "Easy!" each time before you slow down and "Quickly!" or "Hustle!" each time before you speed up, and the dog will learn to change pace on cue. If the dog lags or leads too far, or if she wanders right or left, simply walk quickly in the opposite direction and maybe even run away from the dog and hide.

Practicing is a lot of fun; you can set up a course in your home, yard or park to do this. Indoors, entice the dog to follow upstairs, into a bedroom, into the bathroom, downstairs, around the living room couch, zigzagging between dining room chairs and into the kitchen for dinner. Outdoors, get the dog to follow around park benches, trees, shrubs and along walkways and lines in the grass. (For safety outdoors, it is advisable to attach a long line on the dog, but never exert corrective tension on the line.)

Remember, following has a lot to do with attitude—
your attitude! Most probably your dog will *not* want to
follow Mr. Grumpy Troll with the personality of wilted
lettuce. Lighten up—walk with a jaunty step, whistle a
happy tune, sing, skip and tell jokes to your dog and
she will be right there by your side.

BY YOUR SIDE

It is smart to train the dog to walk close on one side or
the other—either side will do, your choice. When walking, jogging or cycling, it is generally bad news to have
the dog suddenly cut in front of you. In fact, I train my
dogs to walk "By my side" and "Other side"—both very
useful instructions. It is possible to position the dog
fairly accurately by looking to the appropriate side and
clicking your fingers or slapping your thigh on that
side. A precise positioning may be attained by holding
a training lure, such as a chew toy, tennis ball or food
treat. Stop and stand still several times throughout the
walk, just as you would when window shopping or
meeting a friend. Use the lure to make sure the dog
slows down and stays close whenever you stop.

When teaching the dog to heel, we generally want
her to sit in heel position when we stop. Teach heel

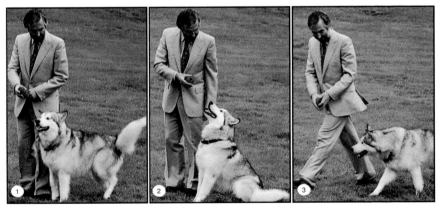

*Using a toy to teach sit-heel-sit sequences: 1) "Phoenix, sit!" Standing still, move lure up and back over dog's
muzzle . . . 2) to position dog sitting in heel position on your left side. 3) Say "Phoenix, heel!" and walk ahead,
wagging lure in left hand. Change lure to right hand in preparation for sit signal. Say "Sit" and then . . .*

position at the standstill and the dog will learn that the default heel position is sitting by your side (left or right—your choice, unless you wish to compete in obedience trials, in which case the dog must heel on the left).

Several times a day, stand up and call your dog to come and sit in heel position—"Tina, heel!" For example, instruct the dog to come to heel each time there are commercials on TV, or each time you turn a page of a novel, and the dog will get it in a single evening.

Practice straight-line heeling and turns separately. With the dog sitting at heel, teach her to turn in place. After each quarter-turn, half-turn or full turn in place, lure the dog to sit at heel. Now it's time for short straight-line heeling sequences, no more than a few steps at a time. Always think of heeling in terms of sit-heel-sit sequences—start and end with the dog in position and do your best to keep her there when moving. Progressively increase the number of steps in each sequence. When the dog remains close for 20 yards of straight-line heeling, it is time to add a few turns and then sign up for a happy-heeling obedience class to get some advice from the experts.

4) use hand signal to lure dog to sit as you stop. Eventually, dog will sit automatically at heel whenever you stop. 5) "Good dog!"

No Pulling on Leash

You can start teaching your dog not to pull on leash anywhere—in front of the television or outdoors—but regardless of location, you must not take a single step with tension in the leash. For a reason known only to dogs, even just a couple of paces of pulling on leash is intrinsically motivating and diabolically rewarding. Instead, attach the leash to the dog's collar, grasp the other end firmly with both hands held close to your chest, and stand still—do not budge an inch. Have somebody watch you with a stopwatch to time your progress, or else you will never believe this will work and so you will not even try the exercise, and your shoulder and the dog's neck will be traumatized for years to come.

Stand still and wait for the dog to stop pulling, and to sit and/or lie down. All dogs stop pulling and sit eventually. Most take only a couple of minutes; the all-time record is 22½ minutes. Time how long it takes. Gently praise the dog when she stops pulling, and as soon as she sits, enthusiastically praise the dog and take just one step forward, then immediately stand still. This single step usually demonstrates the ballistic reinforcing nature of pulling on leash; most dogs explode to the end of the leash, so be prepared for the strain. Stand firm and wait for the dog to sit again. Repeat this half a dozen times and you will probably notice a progressive reduction in the force of the dog's one-step explosions and a radical reduction in the time it takes for the dog to sit each time.

As the dog learns "Sit we go" and "Pull we stop," she will begin to walk forward calmly with each single step and automatically sit when you stop. Now try two steps before you stop. Wooooooo! Scary! When the dog has mastered two steps at a time, try for three. After each success, progressively increase the number of steps in the sequence: try four steps and then six, eight, ten and twenty steps before stopping. Congratulations! You are now walking the dog on leash.

Whenever walking with the dog (off leash or on leash), make sure you stop periodically to practice a few position commands and stays before instructing the dog to "Walk on!" (Remember, you want the dog to be compliant everywhere, not just in the kitchen when her dinner is at hand.) For example, stopping every 25 yards to briefly train the dog amounts to over 200 training interludes within a single 3-mile stroll. And each training session is in a different location. You will not believe the improvement within just the first mile of the first walk.

To put it another way, integrating training into a walk offers 200 separate opportunities to use the continuance of the walk as a reward to reinforce the dog's education. Moreover, some training interludes may comprise continuing education for the dog's walking skills: Alternate short periods of the dog walking calmly by your side with periods when the dog is allowed to sniff and investigate the environment. Now sniffing odors on the grass and meeting other dogs become rewards which reinforce the dog's calm and mannerly demeanor. Good Lord! Whatever next? Many enjoyable walks together of course. Happy trails!

THE IMPORTANCE OF TRICKS

Nothing will improve a dog's quality of life better than having a few tricks under her belt. Teaching any trick expands the dog's vocabulary, which facilitates communication and improves the owner's control. Also, specific tricks help prevent and resolve specific behavior problems. For example, by teaching the dog to fetch her toys, the dog learns carrying a toy makes the owner happy and, therefore, will be more likely to chew her toy than other inappropriate items.

More important, teaching tricks prompts owners to lighten up and train with a sunny disposition. Really, tricks should be no different from any other behaviors we put on cue. But they are. When teaching tricks, owners have a much sweeter attitude, which in turn motivates the dog and improves her willingness to comply. The dog feels tricks are a blast, but formal commands are a drag. In fact, tricks are so enjoyable, they may be used as rewards in training by asking the dog to come, sit and down-stay and then rollover for a tummy rub. Go on, try it: Crack a smile and even giggle when the dog promptly and willingly lies down and stays.

Most important, performing tricks prompts onlookers to smile and giggle. Many people are scared of dogs, especially large ones. And nothing can be more off-putting for a dog than to be constantly confronted by strangers who don't like her because of her size or the way she looks. Uneasy people put the dog on edge, causing her to back off and bark, only frightening people all the more. And so a vicious circle develops, with the people's fear fueling the dog's fear *and vice versa*. Instead, tie a pink ribbon to your dog's collar and practice all sorts of tricks on walks and in the park, and you will be pleasantly amazed how it changes people's attitudes toward your friendly dog. The dog's repertoire of tricks is limited only by the trainer's imagination. Below I have described three of my favorites:

SPEAK AND SHUSH

The training sequence involved in teaching a dog to bark on request is no different from that used when training any behavior on cue: request—lure—response—reward. As always, the secret of success lies in finding an effective lure. If the dog always barks at the doorbell, for example, say "Rover, speak!", have an accomplice ring the doorbell, then reward the dog for barking. After a few woofs, ask Rover to "Shush!", waggle a food treat under her nose (to entice her to sniff and thus to shush), praise her when quiet and eventually offer the treat as a reward. Alternate "Speak" and "Shush," progressively increasing the length of shush-time between each barking bout.

PLAY BOW

With the dog standing, say "Bow!" and lower the food lure (palm upwards) to rest between the dog's forepaws. Praise as the dog lowers her forequarters and sternum to the ground (as when teaching the down), but then lure the dog to stand and offer the treat. On successive trials, gradually increase the length of time the dog is required to remain in the play bow posture in order to gain a food reward. If the dog's rear end collapses into a down, say nothing and offer no reward; simply start over.

BE A BEAR

With the dog sitting backed into a corner to prevent her from toppling over backwards, say "Be a bear!" With bent paw and palm down, raise a lure upwards and backwards along the top of the dog's muzzle. Praise the dog when she sits up on her haunches and offer the treat as a reward. To prevent the dog from standing on her hind legs, keep the lure closer to the dog's muzzle. On each trial, progressively increase the length of time the dog is required to sit up to receive a food reward. Since lure-reward training is so easy, teach the dog to stand and walk on her hind legs as well!

Teaching "Be a Bear"

Getting
Active
with your Dog
by Bardi McLennan

Once you and your dog have graduated from basic obedience training and are beginning to work together as a team, you can take part in the growing world of dog activities. There are so many fun things to do with your dog! Just remember, people and dogs don't always learn at the same pace, so don't be upset if you (or your dog) need more than two basic training courses before your team becomes operational. Even smart dogs don't go straight to college from kindergarten!

Just as there are events geared to certain types of dogs, so there are ones that are more appealing to certain types of people. In some activities, you give the commands and your dog does the work (upland game hunting is one example), while in others, such as agility, you'll both get a workout. You may want to aim for prestigious titles to add to your dog's name, or you may want nothing more than the sheer enjoyment of being around other people and their dogs. Passive or active, participation has its own rewards.

Consider your dog's physical capabilities when looking into any of the canine activities. It's easy to see that a Basset Hound is not built for the racetrack, nor would a Chihuahua be the breed of choice for pulling a sled. A loyal dog will attempt almost anything you ask him to do, so it is up to you to know your dog's limitations. A dog must be physically sound in order to compete at any level in athletic activities, and being mentally sound is a definite plus. Advanced age, however, may not be a deterrent. Many dogs still hunt and herd at ten or twelve years of age. It's entirely possible for dogs to be "fit at 50." Take your dog for a checkup, explain to your vet the type of activity you have in mind and be guided by his or her findings.

All dogs seem to love playing flyball.

You needn't be restricted to breed-specific sports if it's only fun you're after. Certain AKC activities are limited to designated breeds; however, as each new trial, test or sport has grown in popularity, so has the variety of breeds encouraged to participate at a fun level.

But don't shortchange your fun, or that of your dog, by thinking only of the basic function of her breed. Once a dog has learned how to learn, she can be taught to do just about anything as long as the size of the dog is right for the job and you both think it is fun and rewarding. In other words, you are a team.

To get involved in any of the activities detailed in this chapter, look for the names and addresses of the organizations that sponsor them in Chapter 13. You can also ask your breeder or a local dog trainer for contacts.

You can compete in obedience trials with a well trained dog.

Official American Kennel Club Activities

The following tests and trials are some of the events sanctioned by the AKC and sponsored by various dog clubs. Your dog's expertise will be rewarded with impressive titles. You can participate just for fun, or be competitive and go for those awards.

OBEDIENCE

Training classes begin with pups as young as three months of age in kindergarten puppy training, then advance to pre-novice (all exercises on lead) and go on to novice, which is where you'll start off-lead work. In obedience classes dogs learn to sit, stay, heel and come through a variety of exercises. Once you've got the basics down, you can enter obedience trials and work toward earning your dog's first degree, a C.D. (Companion Dog).

The next level is called "Open," in which jumps and retrieves perk up the dog's interest. Passing grades in competition at this level earn a C.D.X. (Companion Dog Excellent). Beyond that lies the goal of the most ambitious—Utility (U.D. and even U.D.X. or OTCh, an Obedience Champion).

AGILITY

All dogs can participate in the latest canine sport to have gained worldwide popularity for its fun and excitement, agility. It began in England as a canine version of horse show-jumping, but because dogs are more agile and able to perform on verbal commands, extra feats were added such as climbing, balancing and racing through tunnels or in and out of weave poles. Many of the obstacles (regulation or homemade) can be set up in your own backyard. If the agility bug bites, you could end up in international competition!

For starters, your dog should be obedience trained, even though, in the beginning, the lessons may all be taught on lead. Once the dog understands the commands (and you do, too), it's as easy as guiding the dog over a prescribed course, one obstacle at a time. In competition, the race is against the clock, so wear your running shoes! The dog starts with 200 points and the judge deducts for infractions and misadventures along the way.

All dogs seem to love agility and respond to it as if they were being turned loose in a playground paradise. Your dog's enthusiasm will be contagious; agility turns into great fun for dog and owner.

FIELD TRIALS AND HUNTING TESTS

There are field trials and hunting tests for the sporting breeds—retrievers, spaniels and pointing breeds, and for some hounds—Bassets, Beagles and Dachshunds. Field trials are competitive events that test a dog's ability to perform the functions for which she was bred. Hunting tests, which are open to retrievers,

---

TITLES AWARDED BY THE AKC

Conformation: Ch. (Champion)

Obedience: CD (Companion Dog); CDX (Companion Dog Excellent); UD (Utility Dog); UDX (Utility Dog Excellent); OTCh. (Obedience Trial Champion)

Field: JH (Junior Hunter); SH (Senior Hunter); MH (Master Hunter); AFCh. (Amateur Field Champion); FCh. (Field Champion)

Lure Coursing: JC (Junior Courser); SC (Senior Courser)

Herding: HT (Herding Tested); PT (Pre-Trial Tested); HS (Herding Started); HI (Herding Intermediate); HX (Herding Excellent); HCh. (Herding Champion)

Tracking: TD (Tracking Dog); TDX (Tracking Dog Excellent)

Agility: NAD (Novice Agility); OAD (Open Agility); ADX (Agility Excellent); MAX (Master Agility)

Earthdog Tests: JE (Junior Earthdog); SE (Senior Earthdog); ME (Master Earthdog)

Canine Good Citizen: CGC

Combination: DC (Dual Champion—Ch. and Fch.); TC (Triple Champion—Ch., Fch., and OTCh.)

spaniels and pointing breeds only, are noncompetitive and are a means of judging the dog's ability as well as that of the handler.

Hunting is a very large and complex part of canine sports, and if you own one of the breeds that hunts, the events are a great treat for your dog and you. He gets to do what he was bred for, and you get to work with him and watch him do it. You'll be proud of and amazed at what your dog can do.

Fortunately, the AKC publishes a series of booklets on these events, which outline the rules and regulations and include a glossary of the sometimes complicated terms. The AKC also publishes newsletters for field trialers and hunting test enthusiasts. The United Kennel Club (UKC) also has informative materials for the hunter and his dog.

Retrievers and other sporting breeds get to do what they're bred to in hunting tests.

HERDING TESTS AND TRIALS

Herding, like hunting, dates back to the first known uses man made of dogs. The interest in herding today is widespread, and if you own a herding breed, you can join in the activity. Herding dogs are tested for their natural skills to keep a flock of ducks, sheep or cattle together. If your dog shows potential, you can start at the testing level, where your dog can earn a title for showing an inherent herding ability. With training you can advance to the trial level, where your dog should be capable of controlling even difficult livestock in diverse situations.

LURE COURSING

The AKC Tests and Trials for Lure Coursing are open to traditional sighthounds—Greyhounds, Whippets,

Borzoi, Salukis, Afghan Hounds, Ibizan Hounds and Scottish Deerhounds—as well as to Basenjis and Rhodesian Ridgebacks. Hounds are judged on overall ability, follow, speed, agility and endurance. This is possibly the most exciting of the trials for spectators, because the speed and agility of the dogs is awesome to watch as they chase the lure (or "course") in heats of two or three dogs at a time.

TRACKING

Tracking is another activity in which almost any dog can compete because every dog that sniffs the ground when taken outdoors is, in fact, tracking. The hard part comes when the rules as to what, when and where the dog tracks are determined by a person, not the dog! Tracking tests cover a large area of fields, woods and roads. The tracks are laid hours before the dogs go to work on them, and include "tricks" like cross-tracks and sharp turns. If you're interested in search-and-rescue work, this is the place to start.

This tracking dog is hot on the trail.

EARTHDOG TESTS FOR SMALL TERRIERS AND DACHSHUNDS

These tests are open to Australian, Bedlington, Border, Cairn, Dandie Dinmont, Smooth and Wire Fox, Lakeland, Norfolk, Norwich, Scottish, Sealyham, Skye, Welsh and West Highland White Terriers as well as Dachshunds. The dogs need no prior training for this terrier sport. There is a qualifying test on the day of the event, so dog and handler learn the rules on the spot. These tests, or "digs," sometimes end with informal races in the late afternoon.

133

Here are some of the extracurricular obedience and racing activities that are not regulated by the AKC or UKC, but are generally run by clubs or a group of dog fanciers and are often open to all.

Canine Freestyle This activity is something new on the scene and is variously likened to dancing, dressage or ice skating. It is meant to show the athleticism of the dog, but also requires showmanship on the part of the dog's handler. If you and your dog like to ham it up for friends, you might want to look into freestyle.

Lure coursing lets sighthounds do what they do best—run!

Scent Hurdle Racing Scent hurdle racing is purely a fun activity sponsored by obedience clubs with members forming competing teams. The height of the hurdles is based on the size of the shortest dog on the team. On a signal, one team dog is released on each of two side-by-side courses and must clear every hurdle before picking up its own dumbbell from a platform and returning over the jumps to the handler. As each dog returns, the next on that team is sent. Of course, that is what the dogs are supposed to do. When the dogs improvise (going under or around the hurdles, stealing another dog's dumbbell, and so forth), it no doubt frustrates the handlers, but just adds to the fun for everyone else.

Flyball This type of racing is similar, but after negotiating the four hurdles, the dog comes to a flyball box, steps on a lever that releases a tennis ball into the air, catches the ball and returns over the hurdles to the starting point. This game also becomes extremely fun for spectators because the dogs sometimes cheat by catching a ball released by the dog in the next lane. Three titles can be earned—Flyball Dog (F.D.), Flyball Dog Excellent (F.D.X.) and Flyball Dog Champion (Fb.D.Ch.)—all awarded by the North American Flyball Association, Inc.

Dogsledding The name conjures up the Rocky Mountains or the frigid North, but you can find dogsled clubs in such unlikely spots as Maryland, North Carolina and Virginia! Dogsledding is primarily for the Nordic breeds such as the Alaskan Malamutes, Siberian Huskies and Samoyeds, but other breeds can try. There are some practical backyard applications to this sport, too. With parental supervision, almost any strong dog could pull a child's sled.

Coming over the A-frame on an agility course.

These are just some of the many recreational ways you can get to know and understand your multifaceted dog better and have fun doing it.

Your Dog
and your
Family

by Bardi McLennan

Adding a dog automatically increases your family by one, no matter whether you live alone in an apartment or are part of a mother, father and six kids household. The single-person family is fair game for numerous and varied canine misconceptions as to who is dog and who pays the bills, whereas a dog in a houseful of children will consider himself to be just one of the gang, littermates all. One dog and one child may give a dog reason to believe they are both kids or both dogs.

Either interpretation requires parental supervision and sometimes speedy intervention.

As soon as one paw goes through the door into your home, Rufus (or Rufina) has to make many adjustments to become a part of your

136

family. Your job is to make him fit in as painlessly as possible. An older dog may have some frame of reference from past experience, but to a 10-week-old puppy, everything is brand new: people, furniture, stairs, when and where people eat, sleep or watch TV, his own place and everyone else's space, smells, sounds, outdoors—everything!

Puppies, and newly acquired dogs of any age, do not need what we think of as "freedom." If you leave a new dog or puppy loose in the house, you will almost certainly return to chaotic destruction and the dog will forever after equate your homecoming with a time of punishment to be dreaded. It is unfair to give your dog what amounts to "freedom to get into trouble." Instead, confine him to a crate for brief periods of your absence (up to three or four hours) and, for the long haul, a workday for example, confine him to one untrashable area with his own toys, a bowl of water and a radio left on (low) in another room.

Lots of pets get along with each other just fine.

For the first few days, when not confined, put Rufus on a long leash tied to your wrist or waist. This umbilical cord method enables the dog to learn all about you from your body language and voice, and to learn by his own actions which things in the house are NO! and which ones are rewarded by "Good dog." Housetraining will be easier with the pup always by your side. Speaking of which, accidents do happen. That goal of "completely housetrained" takes up to a year, or the length of time it takes the pup to mature.

The All-Adult Family

Most dogs in an adults-only household today are likely to be latchkey pets, with no one home all day but the dog. When you return after a tough day on the job, the dog can and should be your relaxation therapy. But going home can instead be a daily frustration.

Separation anxiety is a very common problem for the dog in a working household. It may begin with whines and barks of loneliness, but it will soon escalate into a frenzied destruction derby. That is why it is so important to set aside the time to teach a dog to relax when left alone in his confined area and to understand that he can trust you to return.

Let the dog get used to your work schedule in easy stages. Confine him to one room and go in and out of that room over and over again. Be casual about it. No physical, voice or eye contact. When the pup no longer even notices your comings and goings, leave the house for varying lengths of time, returning to stay home for a few minutes and gradually increasing the time away. This training can take days, but the dog is learning that you haven't left him forever and that he can trust you.

Any time you leave the dog, but especially during this training period, be casual about your departure. No anxiety-building fond farewells. Just "Bye" and go! Remember the "Good dog" when you return to find everything more or less as you left it.

If things are a mess (or even a disaster) when you return, greet the dog, take him outside to eliminate, and then put him in his crate while you clean up. Rant and rave in the shower! *Do not* punish the dog. You were not there when it happened, and the rule is: Only punish as you catch the dog in the act of wrongdoing. Obviously, it makes sense to get your latchkey puppy when you'll have a week or two to spend on these training essentials.

Family weekend activities should include Rufus whenever possible. Depending on the pup's age, now is the time for a long walk in the park, playtime in the backyard, a hike in the woods. Socializing is as important as health care, good food and physical exercise, so visiting Aunt Emma or Uncle Harry and the next-door neighbor's dog or cat is essential to developing an outgoing, friendly temperament in your pet.

If you are a single adult, socializing Rufus at home and away will prevent him from becoming overly protective of you (or just overly attached) and will also prevent such behavioral problems as dominance or fear of strangers.

Babies

Whether already here or on the way, babies figure larger than life in the eyes of a dog. If the dog is there first, let him in on all your baby preparations in the house. When baby arrives, let Rufus sniff any item of clothing that has been on the baby before Junior comes home. Then let Mom greet the dog first before introducing the new family member. Hold the baby down for the dog to see and sniff, but make sure someone's holding the dog on lead in case of any sudden moves. Don't play keep-away or tease the dog with the baby, which only invites undesirable jumping up.

The dog and the baby are "family," and for starters can be treated almost as equals. Things rapidly change, however, especially when baby takes to creeping around on all fours on the dog's turf or, better yet, has yummy pudding all over her face and hands! That's when a lot of things in the dog's and baby's lives become more separate than equal.

Dogs are perfect confidants.

Toddlers make terrible dog owners, but if you can't avoid the combination, use patient discipline (that is, positive teaching rather than punishment), and use time-outs before you run out of patience.

139

A dog and a baby (or toddler, or an assertive young child) should never be left alone together. Take the dog with you or confine him. With a baby or youngsters in the house, you'll have plenty of use for that wonderful canine safety device called a crate!

Young Children

Any dog in a house with kids will behave pretty much as the kids do, good or bad. But even good dogs and good children can get into trouble when play becomes rowdy and active.

Teach children how to play nicely with a puppy.

Legs bobbing up and down, shrill voices screeching, a ball hurtling overhead, all add up to exuberant frustration for a dog who's just trying to be part of the gang. In a pack of puppies, any legs or toys being chased would be caught by a set of teeth, and all the pups involved would understand that is how the game is played. Kids do not understand this, nor do parents tolerate it. Bring Rufus indoors before you have reason to regret it. This is time-out, not a punishment.

You can explain the situation to the children and tell them they must play quieter games until the puppy learns not to grab them with his mouth. Unfortunately, you can't explain it that easily to the dog. With adult supervision, they will learn how to play together.

Young children love to tease. Sticking their faces or wiggling their hands or fingers in the dog's face is teasing. To another person it might be just annoying, but it is threatening to a dog. There's another difference: We can make the child stop by an explanation, but the only way a dog can stop it is with a warning growl and then with teeth. Teasing is the major cause of children being bitten by their pets. Treat it seriously.

Older Children

The best age for a child to get a first dog is between the ages of 8 and 12. That's when kids are able to accept some real responsibility for their pet. Even so, take the child's vow of "I will never *ever* forget to feed (brush, walk, etc.) the dog" for what it's worth: a child's good intention at that moment. Most kids today have extra lessons, soccer practice, Little League, ballet, and so forth piled on top of school schedules. There will be many times when Mom will have to come to the dog's rescue. "I walked the dog for you so you can set the table for me" is one way to get around a missed appointment without laying on blame or guilt.

Kids in this age group make excellent obedience trainers because they are into the teaching/learning process themselves and they lack the self-consciousness of adults. Attending a dog show is something the whole family can enjoy, and watching Junior Showmanship may catch the eye of the kids. Older children can begin to get involved in many of the recreational activities that were reviewed in the previous chapter. Some of the agility obstacles, for example, can be set up in the backyard as a family project (with an adult making sure all the equipment is safe and secure for the dog).

Older kids are also beginning to look to the future, and may envision themselves as veterinarians or trainers or show dog handlers or writers of the next Lassie best-seller. Dogs are perfect confidants for these dreams. They won't tell a soul.

Other Pets

Introduce all pets tactfully. In a dog/cat situation, hold the dog, not the cat. Let two dogs meet on neutral turf—a stroll in the park or a walk down the street—with both on loose leads to permit all the normal canine ways of saying hello, including routine sniffing, circling, more sniffing, and so on. Small creatures such as hamsters, chinchillas or mice must be kept safe from their natural predators (dogs and cats).

Festive Family Occasions

Parties are great for people, but not necessarily for puppies. Until all the guests have arrived, put the dog in his crate or in a room where he won't be disturbed. A socialized dog can join the fun later as long as he's not underfoot, annoying guests or into the hors d'oeuvres.

There are a few dangers to consider, too. Doors opening and closing can allow a puppy to slip out unnoticed in the confusion, and you'll be organizing a search party instead of playing host or hostess. Party food and buffet service are not for dogs. Let Rufus party in his crate with a nice big dog biscuit.

At Christmas time, not only are tree decorations dangerous and breakable (and perhaps family heirlooms), but extreme caution should be taken with the lights, cords and outlets for the tree lights and any other festive lighting. Occasionally a dog lifts a leg, ignoring the fact that the tree is indoors. To avoid this, use a canine repellent, made for gardens, on the tree. Or keep him out of the tree room unless supervised. And whatever you do, *don't* invite trouble by hanging his toys on the tree!

Car Travel

Before you plan a vacation by car or RV with Rufus, be sure he enjoys car travel. Nothing spoils a holiday quicker than a carsick dog! Work within the dog's comfort level. Get in the car with the dog in his crate or attached to a canine car safety belt and just sit there until he relaxes. That's all. Next time, get in the car, turn on the engine and go nowhere. Just sit. When that is okay, turn on the engine and go around the block. Now you can go for a ride and include a stop where you get out, leaving the dog for a minute or two.

On a warm day, always park in the shade and leave windows open several inches. And return quickly. It only takes 10 minutes for a car to become an overheated steel death trap.

Motel or Pet Motel?

Not all motels or hotels accept pets, but you have a much better choice today than even a few years ago. To find a dog-friendly lodging, look at *On the Road Again With Man's Best Friend*, a series of directories that detail bed and breakfasts, inns, family resorts and other hotels/motels. Some places require a refundable deposit to cover any damage incurred by the dog. More B&Bs accept pets now, but some restrict the size.

If taking Rufus with you is not feasible, check out boarding kennels in your area. Your veterinarian may offer this service, or recommend a kennel or two he or she is familiar with. Go see the facilities for yourself, ask about exercise, diet, housing, and so on. Or, if you'd rather have Rufus stay home, look into bonded petsitters, many of whom will also bring in the mail and water your plants.

chapter 11

Your Dog
and your
Community

by Bardi McLennan

Step outside your home with your dog and you are no longer just family, you are both part of your community. This is when the phrase "responsible pet ownership" takes on serious implications. For starters, it means you pick up after your dog—not just occasionally, but every time your dog eliminates away from home. That means you have joined the Plastic Baggy Brigade! You always have plastic sandwich bags in your pocket and several in the car. It means you teach your kids how to use them, too. If you think this is "yucky," just imagine what the person (a non-doggy person) who inadvertently steps in the mess thinks!

Your responsibility extends to your neighbors: To their ears (no annoying barking); to their property (their garbage, their lawn, their flower beds, their cat—especially their cat); to their kids (on bikes, at play); to their kids' toys and sports equipment.

There are numerous dog-related laws, ranging from simple dog licensing and leash laws to those holding you liable for any physical injury or property damage done by your dog. These laws are in place to protect everyone in the community, including you and your dog. There are town ordinances and state laws which are by no means the same in all towns or all states. Ignorance of the law won't get you off the hook. The time to find out what the laws are where you live is now.

Be sure your dog's license is current. This is not just a good local ordinance, it can make the difference between finding your lost dog or not.

Dressing your dog up makes him appealing to strangers.

Many states now require proof of rabies vaccination and that the dog has been spayed or neutered before issuing a license. At the same time, keep up the dog's annual immunizations.

Never let your dog run loose in the neighborhood. This will not only keep you on the right side of the leash law, it's the outdoor version of the rule about not giving your dog "freedom to get into trouble."

Good Canine Citizen

Sometimes it's hard for a dog's owner to assess whether or not the dog is sufficiently socialized to be accepted by the community at large. Does Rufus or Rufina display good, controlled behavior in public? The AKC's Canine Good Citizen program is available through many dog organizations. If your dog passes the test, the title "CGC" is earned.

The overall purpose is to turn your dog into a good neighbor and to teach you about your responsibility to your community as a dog owner. Here are the ten things your dog must do willingly:

1. Accept a stranger stopping to chat with you.
2. Sit and be petted by a stranger.
3. Allow a stranger to handle him or her as a groomer or veterinarian would.
4. Walk nicely on a loose lead.
5. Walk calmly through a crowd.
6. Sit and down on command, then stay in a sit or down position while you walk away.
7. Come when called.
8. Casually greet another dog.
9. React confidently to distractions.
10. Accept being left alone with someone other than you and not become overly agitated or nervous.

Schools and Dogs

Schools are getting involved with pet ownership on an educational level. It has been proven that children who are kind to animals are humane in their attitude toward other people as adults.

A dog is a child's best friend, and so children are often primary pet owners, if not the primary caregivers. Unfortunately, they are also the ones most often bitten by dogs. This occurs due to a lack of understanding that pets, no matter how sweet, cuddly and loving, are still animals. Schools, along with parents, dog clubs, dog fanciers and the AKC, are working to change all that with video programs for children not only in grade school, but in the nursery school and pre-kindergarten age group. Teaching youngsters how to be responsible dog owners is important community work. When your dog has a CGC, volunteer to take part in an educational classroom event put on by your dog club.

Boy Scout Merit Badge

A Merit Badge for Dog Care can be earned by any Boy Scout ages 11 to 18. The requirements are not easy, but amount to a complete course in responsible dog care and general ownership. Here are just a few of the things a Scout must do to earn that badge:

Point out ten parts of the dog using the correct names.

Give a report (signed by parent or guardian) on your care of the dog (feeding, food used, housing, exercising, grooming and bathing), plus what has been done to keep the dog healthy.

Explain the right way to obedience train a dog, and demonstrate three comments.

Several of the requirements have to do with health care, including first aid, handling a hurt dog, and the dangers of home treatment for a serious ailment.

The final requirement is to know the local laws and ordinances involving dogs.

There are similar programs for Girl Scouts and 4-H members.

Local Clubs

Local dog clubs are no longer in existence just to put on a yearly dog show. Today, they are apt to be the hub of the community's involvement with pets. Dog clubs conduct educational forums with big-name speakers, stage demonstrations of canine talent in a busy mall and take dogs of various breeds to schools for class-room discussion.

The quickest way to feel accepted as a member in a club is to volunteer your services! Offer to help with something—anything—and watch your popularity (and your interest) grow.

Therapy Dogs

Once your dog has earned that essential CGC and reliably demonstrates a steady, calm temperament, you could look into what therapy dogs are doing in your area.

Therapy dogs go with their owners to visit patients at hospitals or nursing homes, generally remaining on leash but able to coax a pat from a stiffened hand, a smile from a blank face, a few words from sealed lips or a hug from someone in need of love.

Nursing homes cover a wide range of patient care. Some specialize in care of the elderly, some in the treatment of specific illnesses, some in physical therapy. Children's facilities also welcome visits from trained therapy dogs for boosting morale in their pediatric patients. Hospice care for the terminally ill and the at-home care of AIDS patients are other areas where this canine visiting is desperately needed. Therapy dog training comes first.

Your dog can make a differ-ence in lots of lives.

There is a lot more involved than just taking your nice friendly pooch to someone's bedside. Doing therapy dog work involves your own emotional stability as well as that of your dog. But once you have met all the requirements for this work, making the rounds once a week or once a month with your therapy dog is possibly the most rewarding of all community activities.

Disaster Aid

This community service is definitely not for everyone, partly because it is time-consuming. The initial training is rigorous, and there can be no let-up in the continuing workouts, because members are on call 24 hours a day to go wherever they are needed at a moment's notice. But if you think you would like to be able to assist in a disaster, look into search-and-rescue work. The network of search-and-rescue volunteers is worldwide, and all members of the American Rescue Dog Association (ARDA) who are qualified to do this work are volunteers who train and maintain their own dogs.

Physical Aid

Most people are familiar with Seeing Eye dogs, which serve as blind people's eyes, but not with all the other work that dogs are trained to do to assist the disabled. Dogs are also specially trained to pull wheelchairs, carry school books, pick up dropped objects, open and close doors. Some also are ears for the deaf. All these assistance-trained dogs, by the way, are allowed anywhere "No Pet" signs exist (as are therapy dogs when

Making the rounds with your therapy dog can be very rewarding.

properly identified). Getting started in any of this fascinating work requires a background in dog training and canine behavior, but there are also volunteer jobs ranging from answering the phone to cleaning out kennels to providing a foster home for a puppy. You have only to ask.

part four

Beyond the Basics

chapter 12

Recommended Reading

Books

ABOUT HEALTH CARE

Ackerman, Lowell. *Guide to Skin and Haircoat Problems in Dogs.* Loveland, Colo.: Alpine Publications, 1994.

Alderton, David. *The Dog Care Manual.* Hauppauge, N.Y.: Barron's Educational Series, Inc., 1986.

American Kennel Club. *American Kennel Club Dog Care and Training.* New York: Howell Book House, 1991.

Bamberger, Michelle, DVM. *Help! The Quick Guide to First Aid for Your Dog.* New York: Howell Book House, 1995.

Carlson, Delbert, DVM, and James Giffin, MD. *Dog Owner's Home Veterinary Handbook.* New York: Howell Book House, 1992.

DeBitetto, James, DVM, and Sarah Hodgson. *You & Your Puppy.* New York: Howell Book House, 1995.

Humphries, Jim, DVM. *Dr. Jim's Animal Clinic for Dogs.* New York: Howell Book House, 1994.

McGinnis, Terri. *The Well Dog Book.* New York: Random House, 1991.

Pitcairn, Richard and Susan. *Natural Health for Dogs.* Emmaus, Pa.: Rodale Press, 1982.

ABOUT DOG SHOWS

Hall, Lynn. *Dog Showing for Beginners.* New York: Howell Book House, 1994.

Nichols, Virginia Tuck. *How to Show Your Own Dog.* Neptune, N. J.: TFH, 1970.

Vanacore, Connie. *Dog Showing, An Owner's Guide.* New York: Howell Book House, 1990.

ABOUT TRAINING

Ammen, Amy. *Training in No Time.* New York: Howell Book House, 1995.

Baer, Ted. *Communicating With Your Dog.* Hauppauge, N.Y.: Barron's Educational Series, Inc., 1989.

Benjamin, Carol Lea. *Dog Problems.* New York: Howell Book House, 1989.

Benjamin, Carol Lea. *Dog Training for Kids.* New York: Howell Book House, 1988.

Benjamin, Carol Lea. *Mother Knows Best.* New York: Howell Book House, 1985.

Benjamin, Carol Lea. *Surviving Your Dog's Adolescence.* New York: Howell Book House, 1993.

Bohnenkamp, Gwen. *Manners for the Modern Dog.* San Francisco: Perfect Paws, 1990.

Dibra, Bashkim. *Dog Training by Bash.* New York: Dell, 1992.

Dunbar, Ian, PhD, MRCVS. *Dr. Dunbar's Good Little Dog Book,* James & Kenneth Publishers, 2140 Shattuck Ave. #2406, Berkeley, Calif. 94704. (510) 658–8588. Order from the publisher.

Dunbar, Ian, PhD, MRCVS. *How to Teach a New Dog Old Tricks,* James & Kenneth Publishers. Order from the publisher; address above.

Dunbar, Ian, PhD, MRCVS, and Gwen Bohnenkamp. Booklets on *Preventing Aggression; Housetraining; Chewing; Digging; Barking; Socialization; Fearfulness; and Fighting,* James & Kenneth Publishers. Order from the publisher; address above.

Evans, Job Michael. *People, Pooches and Problems.* New York: Howell Book House, 1991.

Kilcommons, Brian and Sarah Wilson. *Good Owners, Great Dogs.* New York: Warner Books, 1992.

McMains, Joel M. *Dog Logic—Companion Obedience.* New York: Howell Book House, 1992.

Rutherford, Clarice and David H. Neil, MRCVS. *How to Raise a Puppy You Can Live With.* Loveland, Colo.: Alpine Publications, 1982.

Volhard, Jack and Melissa Bartlett. *What All Good Dogs Should Know: The Sensible Way to Train.* New York: Howell Book House, 1991.

ABOUT BREEDING

Harris, Beth J. Finder. *Breeding a Litter, The Complete Book of Prenatal and Postnatal Care.* New York: Howell Book House, 1983.

Holst, Phyllis, DVM. *Canine Reproduction.* Loveland, Colo.: Alpine Publications, 1985.

Walkowicz, Chris and Bonnie Wilcox, DVM. *Successful Dog Breeding, The Complete Handbook of Canine Midwifery*. New York: Howell Book House, 1994.

ABOUT ACTIVITIES

American Rescue Dog Association. *Search and Rescue Dogs*. New York: Howell Book House, 1991.

Barwig, Susan and Stewart Hilliard. *Schutzhund*. New York: Howell Book House, 1991.

Beaman, Arthur S. *Lure Coursing*. New York: Howell Book House, 1994.

Daniels, Julie. *Enjoying Dog Agility—From Backyard to Competition*. New York: Doral Publishing, 1990.

Davis, Kathy Diamond. *Therapy Dogs*. New York: Howell Book House, 1992.

Gallup, Davis Anne. *Running With Man's Best Friend*. Loveland, Colo.: Alpine Publications, 1986.

Habgood, Dawn and Robert. *On the Road Again With Man's Best Friend*. New England, Mid-Atlantic, West Coast and Southeast editions. Selective guides to area bed and breakfasts, inns, hotels and resorts that welcome guests and their dogs. New York: Howell Book House, 1995.

Holland, Vergil S. *Herding Dogs*. New York: Howell Book House, 1994.

LaBelle, Charlene G. *Backpacking With Your Dog*. Loveland, Colo.: Alpine Publications, 1993.

Simmons-Moake, Jane. *Agility Training, The Fun Sport for All Dogs*. New York: Howell Book House, 1991.

Spencer, James B. *Hup! Training Flushing Spaniels the American Way*. New York: Howell Book House, 1992.

Spencer, James B. *Point! Training the All-Seasons Birddog*. New York: Howell Book House, 1995.

Tarrant, Bill. *Training the Hunting Retriever*. New York: Howell Book House, 1991.

Volhard, Jack and Wendy. *The Canine Good Citizen*. New York: Howell Book House, 1994.

General Titles

Haggerty, Captain Arthur J. *How to Get Your Pet Into Show Business*. New York: Howell Book House, 1994.

McLennan, Bardi. *Dogs and Kids, Parenting Tips*. New York: Howell Book House, 1993.

Moran, Patti J. *Pet Sitting for Profit, A Complete Manual for Professional Success*. New York: Howell Book House, 1992.

Scalisi, Danny and Libby Moses. *When Rover Just Won't Do, Over 2,000 Suggestions for Naming Your Dog.* New York: Howell Book House, 1993.

Sife, Wallace, PhD. *The Loss of a Pet.* New York: Howell Book House, 1993.

Wrede, Barbara J. *Civilizing Your Puppy.* Hauppauge, N.Y.: Barron's Educational Series, 1992.

Magazines

The AKC GAZETTE, The Official Journal for the Sport of Purebred Dogs. American Kennel Club, 51 Madison Ave., New York, NY.

Bloodlines Journal. United Kennel Club, 100 E. Kilgore Rd., Kalamazoo, MI.

Dog Fancy. Fancy Publications, 3 Burroughs, Irvine, CA 92718

Dog World. Maclean Hunter Publishing Corp., 29 N. Wacker Dr., Chicago, IL 60606.

Videos

"SIRIUS Puppy Training," by Ian Dunbar, PhD, MRCVS. James & Kenneth Publishers, 2140 Shattuck Ave. #2406, Berkeley, CA 94704. Order from the publisher.

"Training the Companion Dog," from Dr. Dunbar's British TV Series, James & Kenneth Publishers. (See address above).

The American Kennel Club produces videos on every breed of dog, as well as on hunting tests, field trials and other areas of interest to purebred dog owners. For more information, write to AKC/Video Fulfillment, 5580 Centerview Dr., Suite 200, Raleigh, NC 27606.

Resources

Breed Clubs

Every breed recognized by the American Kennel Club has a national (parent) club. National clubs are a great source of information on your breed. You can get the name of the secretary of the club by contacting:

The American Kennel Club
51 Madison Avenue
New York, NY 10010
(212) 696-8200

There are also numerous all-breed, individual breed, obedience, hunting and other special-interest dog clubs across the country. The American Kennel Club can provide you with a geographical list of clubs to find ones in your area. Contact them at the above address.

Registry Organizations

Registry organizations register purebred dogs. The American Kennel Club is the oldest and largest in this country, and currently recognizes over 130 breeds. The United Kennel Club registers some breeds the AKC doesn't (including the American Pit Bull Terrier and the Miniature Fox Terrier) as well as many of the same breeds. The others included here are for your reference; the AKC can provide you with a list of foreign registries.

American Kennel Club
51 Madison Avenue
New York, NY 10010

United Kennel Club (UKC)
100 E. Kilgore Road
Kalamazoo, MI 49001-5598

American Dog Breeders Assn.
P.O. Box 1771
Salt Lake City, UT 84110
(Registers American Pit Bull Terriers)

Canadian Kennel Club
89 Skyway Avenue
Etobicoke, Ontario
Canada M9W 6R4

National Stock Dog Registry
P.O. Box 402
Butler, IN 46721
(Registers working stock dogs)

Orthopedic Foundation for Animals (OFA)
2300 E. Nifong Blvd.
Columbia, MO 65201-3856
(Hip registry)

Activity Clubs

Write to these organizations for information on the
activities they sponsor.

American Kennel Club
51 Madison Avenue
New York, NY 10010
(Conformation Shows, Obedience Trials, Field
Trials and Hunting Tests, Agility, Canine Good

Citizen, Lure Coursing, Herding, Tracking,
Earthdog Tests, Coonhunting.)

United Kennel Club
100 E. Kilgore Road
Kalamazoo, MI 49001-5598
(Conformation Shows, Obedience Trials, Agility,
Hunting for Various Breeds, Terrier Trials and
more.)

North American Flyball Assn.
1342 Jeff St.
Ypsilanti, MI 48198

International Sled Dog Racing Assn.
P.O. Box 446
Norman, ID 83848-0446

North American Working Dog Assn., Inc.
Southeast Kreisgruppe
P.O. Box 833
Brunswick, GA 31521

Trainers

Association of Pet Dog Trainers
P.O. Box 385
Davis, CA 95617
(800) PET–DOGS

American Dog Trainers' Network
161 West 4th St.
New York, NY 10014
(212) 727–7257

**National Association of Dog Obedience
Instructors**
2286 East Steel Rd.
St. Johns, MI 48879

Associations

American Dog Owners Assn.
1654 Columbia Tpk.
Castleton, NY 12033
(Combats anti-dog legislation)

Delta Society
P.O. Box 1080
Renton, WA 98057-1080
(Promotes the human/animal bond through
pet-assisted therapy and other programs)

Dog Writers Assn. of America (DWAA)
Sally Cooper, Secy.
222 Woodchuck Ln.
Harwinton, CT 06791

National Assn. for Search and Rescue (NASAR)
P.O. Box 3709
Fairfax, VA 22038

Therapy Dogs International
6 Hilltop Road
Mendham, NJ 07945